my revision notes

WJEC and Eduqas A level

RELIGIOUS STUDIES

Religion and Ethics

Clare Lloyd

HODDER EDUCATION
AN HACHETTE UK COMPANY

The Publishers would like to thank the following for permission to reproduce copyright material.

Acknowledgements

Bible quotations taken from New Revised Standard Version Bible: Anglicized Edition, copyright © 1989, 1995 National Council of the Churches of Christ in the United States of America. Used by permission. All rights reserved worldwide.

Every effort has been made to trace all copyright holders, but if any have been inadvertently overlooked, the Publishers will be pleased to make the necessary arrangements at the first opportunity.

Although every effort has been made to ensure that website addresses are correct at time of going to press, Hodder Education cannot be held responsible for the content of any website mentioned in this book. It is sometimes possible to find a relocated web page by typing in the address of the home page for a website in the URL window of your browser.

Hachette UK's policy is to use papers that are natural, renewable and recyclable products and made from wood grown in well-managed forests and other controlled sources. The logging and manufacturing processes are expected to conform to the environmental regulations of the country of origin.

Orders: please contact Bookpoint Ltd, 130 Park Drive, Milton Park, Abingdon, Oxon OX14 4SE. Telephone: +44 (0)1235 827827. Fax: +44 (0)1235 400401. Email education@bookpoint.co.uk Lines are open from 9 a.m. to 5 p.m., Monday to Saturday, with a 24-hour message answering service. You can also order through our website: www.hoddereducation.co.uk

ISBN: 978 1 5104 5051 6

© Clare Lloyd 2019
First published in 2019 by
Hodder Education,
An Hachette UK Company
Carmelite House
50 Victoria Embankment
London EC4Y 0DZ

www.hoddereducation.co.uk

Impression number   10 9 8 7 6 5 4 3
Year   2023 2022 2021 2020

Illustrations by Aptara, Inc.

Typeset in Bembo Std Regular 11/13pt by Aptara, Inc.

Printed in India by Replika Press Pvt. Ltd.

A catalogue record for this title is available from the British Library.

My revision planner

WJEC/Eduqas mapping table

The content of the Ethics specification does not differ between WJEC and Eduqas although the codes for each unit are different. The structure of examination papers does differ slightly and so the following chart indicates the significant similarities and differences.

WJEC	Eduqas
AS	**AS**
One paper for an Introduction to Religion and Ethics and an Introduction to the Philosophy of Religion	Two separate papers for an Introduction to Religion and Ethics and an Introduction to the Philosophy of Religion
Each paper takes 1 hour 45 minutes	Each paper takes 1 hour 30 minutes
The whole paper is split into two halves	The whole paper is split into two halves
Section A tests Ethics and Section B tests Philosophy. Each has two questions	Section A has two questions and Section B has three questions
You must answer one question from each section	You must answer one question from each section
Each question is split into part A (AO1) and part B (AO2)	Each question is split into part A (AO1) and part B (AO2)
Each part is worth 30 marks	Each part is worth 25 marks
Part A (AO1) tests knowledge and understanding, part B (AO2) tests analysis and evaluation	Part A (AO1) tests knowledge and understanding, part B (AO2) tests analysis and evaluation
A Level	**A Level**
Two separate papers for Religion and Ethics and Philosophy of Religion	Two separate papers for Religion and Ethics and Philosophy of Religion
Each paper takes 1 hour 30 minutes	Each paper takes 2 hours
The whole paper is split into two halves	The whole paper is split into two halves
Section A has two questions and Section B has four questions	Section A has two questions and Section B has three questions
You must answer one question from Section A and two from Section B	You must answer one question from each section
The questions are not split into parts	Each question is split into part A (AO1) and part B (AO2)
Each question is worth 30 marks	Part A is worth 20 marks and part B is worth 30 marks
Section A (AO1) of the paper tests knowledge and understanding, Section B (AO2) tests analysis and evaluation	Part A (AO1) tests knowledge and understanding, part B (AO2) tests analysis and evaluation

Theme 1 Ethical thought

The word 'ethics' comes from the Greek 'ethike', which means habit or behaviour. The study of ethics is the consideration of guiding principles that direct our actions. There are four ways of studying ethics.

Meta-ethics	Literally: beyond ethics. This branch of ethics studies the meaning of ethical language and the foundations and scope of ethical knowledge.
Normative ethics	Comes up with the systems and procedures for judging moral acts as right or wrong and for regulating moral action.
Descriptive ethics	Passes no judgement but recounts the ethical behaviour of communities or individuals.
Applied ethics	Puts normative theories into practice in real-life situations.

Typical mistake

Don't muddle meta-ethics (how we understand the meaning of ethical words) with normative ethics (how we should act ethically).

1A Divine Command Theory

Divine Command Theory (**Theological Voluntarism**) says it is our duty to obey rules that are commanded by God. Any acts that are forbidden by God are necessarily bad or wrong.

Meta-ethical theory – God as the origin and regulator of morality

REVISED

This theory claims that moral knowledge is possible and **objective**. We can understand clearly what is right and wrong with reference to what God commands. So, ethics is not **relative** to the preferences of culture. It is **absolute**.

It is dependent upon the **theistic** claim that there is one God who is:

Omnibenevolent	All-loving and compassionate
Omnipotent	All-powerful
Omniscient	All-knowing
Omnipresent	Present everywhere

God has created all things, including the law. In Genesis, it claims that everything God made was good.

> 'God saw everything that he had made, and indeed, it was very good.'
> Genesis 1:31 (NRSV)

God also has issued his law through the scriptures, which clearly declare the moral code that is to be followed.

> 'All scripture is inspired by God and is useful for teaching, for reproof, for correction and for training in righteousness, so that everyone who belongs to God may be proficient, equipped for every good work.'
> 2 Timothy 3:16–17 (NRSV)

Theological Voluntarism – another name for Divine Command Theory.

Objective – factual and uninfluenced by opinion.

Relative – without binding laws, dependent upon context or situation.

Absolute – universally valid, unaltered by reference to other factors.

Theistic – belief in one God as creator and sustainer of the universe.

Right or wrong as objective truths based on God's will/command

REVISED

God's commands are a standard for moral behaviour. Right is right only because God has commanded it and wrong is wrong only because it is forbidden by God. Moral actions are defined by God's will. These rules apply **universally**, regardless of time and culture. This objective standard originates from God rather than being something external to him.

Universal – applicable in all cases.

Moral goodness is achieved by complying with divine command

REVISED

A moral agent must obey the commands laid out by God, by following the commandments in scripture or church teaching. In normative terms, such a theory is **deontological** since it becomes the duty of the moral agent to obey God's commands. Our relationship with God is vital for ethical behaviour because those in fellowship with God can better understand his will.

Deontological – from the Greek 'deon', meaning duty or obligation.

Now test yourself

TESTED

1 What four qualities do theists claim God has?
2 How can I know what is good according to Divine Command Theory?
3 What is the meaning of the words deontological and universal?
4 How can I find out what God commands?

Divine command as a requirement of God's omnipotence

REVISED

If God is truly all-powerful, it is vital that he is not controlled or subject to the power of morality. If God's goodness was because of his obedience to law, then the rules would be a higher authority than God. To understand God as truly omnipotent, we must comprehend him to be the origin of both goodness and commands.

Divine command as an objective meta-physical foundation for morality

REVISED

Biblical writers viewed morality theologically. This means that they saw the origin of morality not as from us but from within the nature and activity of God. The definition of the word right is simply 'commanded by God' and wrong is 'forbidden by God'. Such rules are the foundation for all ethical behaviour. No circumstances or good intentions can make acts that are forbidden by God right.

Meta-physical – relating to non-physical concepts, e.g. time, being or the qualities of God.

Who is Robert Adams?
Robert Adams (1937–present day) is an American philosopher who has taught at UCLA, Yale and the University of Oxford as professor of moral philosophy and meta-physics. Among his works is an essay entitled 'A Modified Divine Command Theory of Ethical Wrongness' (1981).

Robert Adams' Modified Divine Command Theory

Adams says that the following statements are the same:

1 It is wrong to steal.

2 Stealing is against God's commands.

Morality is not simply based on a command from God. It is **intrinsic** to his unchanging omnibenevolent nature. Moral goodness is not **arbitrary** or cruel because God's nature is intrinsically, unfailingly benevolent. To command anything that is not good would be a violation of God's nature and essence. While it is not logically impossible for a loving God to command cruelty, it is unthinkable given God's nature. Since morality is an essential characteristic of God, anything moral will always reflect God's character.

> **Intrinsic** – essential to or belonging naturally to; as part of the character of.
>
> **Arbitrary** – random, without reason.

> **Revision activity**
>
> Make some 'Flappable Flashcards'. Fold an index card in half widthways. On the front, write three 'test yourself' style questions and write the answers inside. Get a revision buddy to test you, or test yourself.

Now test yourself

TESTED

1 Who developed the Modified Divine Command Theory?
2 What does arbitrary mean?
3 Why can't God command anything arbitrary?

Challenges

REVISED

The Euthyphro dilemma

The Euthyphro dilemma is a challenge to the Divine Command Theory that dates back to Plato's work *The Last Days of Socrates*, in which is found a dialogue entitled Euthyphro. Euthyphro and Socrates discuss how we know what holiness is. Here, Socrates states the dilemma:

Is the holy approved by the gods because it is holy?	Is the holy holy because it is approved by the gods?
The gods are only good because they live up to an independent standard. They are no longer the ultimate moral authority. For example, God sees that truthfulness is right, but he doesn't make it right. Why should we obey God then?	The gods can approve of and command anything they like, and it would be good because it is approved of by them. They could call lying good and it would be. This doesn't sound like a god worth worshipping.

Robert Adams' Modified Divine Command Theory attempts to resolve this problem by understanding goodness as being at the heart of God's nature rather than external to him (extrinsic) or arbitrary.

Arbitrariness problem

The second 'horn' of the Euthyphro dilemma is sometimes called the arbitrariness problem. If the definition of good is that it is approved of by God, he can command something random and declare it good. This means that whatever God declares good does not have to have any special quality that allows it to be judged this way. The goodness of such an act is purely because God has decreed it.

Robert Adams attempts to resolve this by understanding that God cannot command a random thing as good since it would be against his intrinsically and supremely good nature to do so.

Pluralism objection

There are many ethical systems around the globe that claim authority with reference to God, or gods. Some of these systems conflict. How do we know which system is right? Such systems have some features in common, but they have differences too. Even if we could establish one clear ethic, there are different interpretations of how laws are meant or applied. For example, Christian teaching forbids divorce in Matthew 5:32, yet allows it in Deuteronomy 24.

Apply your knowledge

Look at the following commandments from the Bible.
- 'You shall not profit by the blood of your neighbour' – Leviticus 19:16
- 'You shall not sow your field with two kinds of seed' – Leviticus 19:19
- '(He must not) return the people to Egypt to acquire more horses' – Deuteronomy 17:16

What could such commands imply about the qualities of God and what it means to be good?

Exam checklist

Can you:
- define meta-ethics, omnipotent, omnibenevolence and Theological Voluntarism
- explain the definition of 'good' and 'bad' according to Divine Command Theory
- explain the challenges of Euthyphro, arbitrariness and pluralism
- state how Adams' Modified Divine Command Theory is different
- define and use terms like objective, absolute, intrinsic, universal and arbitrary in your work?

Revision activity

Try making a timeline of scholars as you work through this revision guide. It will help you remember who's who. Don't forget to include which theory they contribute to.

Typical mistake

Some students answer the question they want rather than the one in front of them. Check the question carefully. Don't write all you know about Divine Command Theory if the question asks for challenges.

1B Virtue Theory

Ethical system based on defining the personal qualities that make a person moral

REVISED

Virtue Ethics is a normative theory that takes a different approach to other normative theories. While most will ask the question 'How should I behave?', Virtue Ethics asks: 'What kind of person should I be?' Virtue Theory is an assessment of the kinds of personal qualities that contribute to making a good person, rather than a system of rules and laws.

Who was Aristotle?
Aristotle (384–322BCE) was an ancient Greek philosopher, a student of Plato, who was responsible for the foundations of modern western thought. As an **empiricist**, he valued reason as applied to the physical world. He is known in ethics for his work *Nichomachean Ethics* (350BCE).

> **Empiricist** – a person who claims that all knowledge comes from sense experience.

The focus on a person's character rather than their specific actions

REVISED

Virtue Theory is based on the Greek word for virtue: **arete**. Virtue Theory is **teleological** in that it considers the purpose of ethics being to achieve a good character by considering our mental state rather than the acts we perform. Virtue is achieved by mimicking or following the example of other ethical people in order to develop the same desirable character traits.

Some people will naturally find it easier than others to develop a virtuous character. Aristotle talks of three kinds of people:

> **Arete** – excellence or moral virtue.
>
> **Teleological** – Greek (telos), meaning end, goal or purpose. A moral theory will consider the purpose of moral behaviour to decide whether it is good.

The Sophron	The Enkrates	The Akrates
Finds it easy to be moderate with little effort	Must work hard but can achieve virtue	Very weak-willed and cannot overcome temptation

Aristotle's moral virtues

REVISED

We always act for a purpose. According to Aristotle, this purpose is to achieve **Eudaemonia**. This word is best translated as well-being or flourishing but is sometimes called happiness. It is the only thing that we want for its own sake. When we desire things for other reasons, eventually they all lead back to the fact that we want to be happy.

> **Eudaemonia** – happiness, well-being, human flourishing.

According to Aristotle, there are three kinds of happiness, all of which are needed to achieve Eudaemonia:
1 Happiness as an individual
2 Happiness as a member of a community
3 Happiness as a philosopher

To achieve Eudaemonia, it is necessary to develop qualities of character that will help you to be content and live in harmony with others. These character traits are known as virtues and there are two different kinds: intellectual and moral. The moral virtues are non-rational and are virtues of character. The intellectual virtues are rational and contribute most to the good life; some relate to theoretical reasoning (What happened in the past? What will happen next?), others to practical reasoning (What should I do?).

Now test yourself answers at **www.hoddereducation.co.uk/myrevisionnotesdownloads**

Intellectual virtues

1 Scientific knowledge
2 Art or technical skill
3 Prudence or practical wisdom
4 Intelligence or intuition
5 Wisdom

Aristotle also explores other areas of intellectual virtue such as resourcefulness, understanding and judgement.

The moral virtues

These 12 virtues each fall between two vices of excess and deficiency. The virtues are known as the **Golden Mean**. This is the middle path between two vices that is the way of moderation.

> **Golden Mean** – the middle, moderate character traits between two vices of excess and deficiency.

Vice of deficiency	Virtue (the Golden Mean)	Vice of excess
Cowardice	Courage	Rashness
Insensibility (no awareness or concern)	Temperance (moderation)	Licentiousness (uncontrolled, especially sexually)
Illiberality (gathers money but doesn't spend)	Liberality (generosity in small amounts of money)	Prodigality (over-spends and under-receives)
Parsimony (miserliness)	Munificence (generosity in large amounts of money)	Vulgarity (flamboyant with money)
Pusillanimity (afraid to stand up for themselves)	Magnanimity (generous in forgiving)	Vainglorious (vanity)
Want of ambition	Right ambition (in small honours)	Over-ambition
Spiritlessness (unconcerned)	Good temper (patience)	Irascibility (easily angered)
Surliness (understatement)	Friendliness	Obsequiousness (overly flattering)
Ironical depreciation (undervaluing)	Sincerity (truthfulness)	Boastfulness
Boorishness (bad-mannered/coarse)	Wittiness	Buffoonery (ridiculous)
Shamelessness	Modesty	Bashfulness
Callousness (malicious enjoyment)	Just resentment (righteous indignation)	Spitefulness (envy)

We learn these moral virtues through developing them as habits. The best learning is through doing. We are what we repeatedly do and so we become courageous by performing courageous acts.

> **Revision tip**
>
> Imagine the 12 virtues as memes. Create your own meme to represent each characteristic.

Now test yourself

TESTED ☐

1 How does Virtue Ethics differ from other normative theories?
2 What is the purpose of human action?
3 How will we learn how to be virtuous?
4 Name and define three virtues and their vices.
5 What is the Golden Mean?

> **Typical mistake**
>
> Don't confuse the Golden Mean (the middle list of virtues between two sets of vices) with the Golden Rule (from Christian Ethics – do to others as you would have them do to you).

Jesus' teachings on virtues

In the New Testament, Matthew presents Jesus giving a long speech that has become known as The Sermon on the Mount. In Matthew 5:3–12, Jesus lists eight moral virtues. These have become known as the **beatitudes**.

> **Beatitudes** – (beautiful attitudes), supreme blessedness or grace.

Each virtue begins with the word 'blessed' and each virtue is promised a reward.

	Virtue	Reward
1	**Poor in spirit** (humbleness)	Kingdom of Heaven
2	**Mourn** (sadness due to separation or loss)	Comfort
3	**Meek** (submissive/gentle)	The earth
4	**Hunger and thirst for righteousness** (seeking justice)	Will be filled
5	**Merciful** (compassionate or forgiving)	Shown mercy
6	**Pure in heart** (sincere intentions)	Will see God
7	**Peacemakers** (bringing reconciliation)	Called the children of God
8	**Persecuted for being righteous** (suffer for standing by their principles)	Kingdom of Heaven

This is not the only mention of virtue in the Bible:

> **1 Corinthians 13:13** St Paul prioritises the virtues of faith, hope and love, claiming that they are superior to any other actions and giving primacy to love.
> **Galatians 5:22–23** St Paul lists love, joy, peace, patience, kindness, goodness, faithfulness, gentleness and self-control as virtues or fruits of the spirit.
> **Micah 6:8** in the Old Testament tells us that God requires us to live justly, love mercy and walk humbly with God.

Revision activity

Compare the lists from Aristotle and Jesus. There are some similarities and some differences. Create a chart that shows where they converge or differ. (Note: Would any of Jesus' virtues seem like vices to Aristotle?)

Typical mistake

Aristotle and Jesus lived 300 years apart. Avoid talking about them as though they knew each other or were contemporaries.

Now test yourself

TESTED

1 List three virtues from Matthew and their respective rewards.
2 Give the scriptural reference where the beatitudes can be found.

Challenges

Virtues are not a practical guide to moral behaviour

- There are no instructions regarding how to behave in specific situations.
- We have no way of knowing whether we have achieved virtue or are still exhibiting vice.
- These virtues are old-fashioned and do not help with modern dilemmas.
- They are romantic and idealistic rather than practical. How do we legislate for this?
- Circular idea: to be virtuous you should do good things; to do good things you should be virtuous.

Issue of cultural relativism

- The list of virtues might differ according to culture or ages (Aristotle recognised this).
- What is moderate in one culture might not seem moderate in another.
- Aristotle's virtues and Christ's list of virtues contradict each other in places.
- Virtue doesn't condemn any act, so it may force us to tolerate terrible acts.
- There is no clear method to decide who is more virtuous.

Virtues can be used for immoral acts

- Virtue could consider it courageous to kill another person, yet killing is wrong in most systems.
- Immoral acts could be performed due to difference of opinion or misuse of virtues.
- Virtue leads to subjugation of women by teaching them 'feminine' virtues that benefit men.
- It focuses on style (the way we are moral) over substance (what is moral).
- Virtue prioritises the needs of humans and ignores the needs of animals or the environment.

Apply your knowledge

1 Amelia and Bryony are best friends. It is Amelia's birthday and Bryony finds Amelia's boyfriend cheating on her with another girl at her birthday party. What is the virtuous thing for Bryony to do?
2 What problems did you discover when making this moral decision according to Virtue Theory?

Exam checklist

Can you:
- define virtue
- explain how this normative theory differs from other theories
- explain the purpose of moral action
- list Aristotle's moral virtues and vices
- list his intellectual virtues
- explain the Golden Mean
- state the location of Jesus' speech on virtues
- list and define the eight virtues from Jesus
- explain the similarities and differences between Aristotle's and Jesus' lists
- explain each of the three types of challenges to virtue?

1C Ethical Egoism

Normative agent focused ethic based on self-interest as opposed to altruism

REVISED

As a normative ethic, egoism is teleological, with the goal of achieving one's own self-interest. This contrasts with **altruism**, which has the good of others as its goal. Egoism says that the only duty a moral agent has is to themselves.

> **Altruism** – selfless concern for others.

In the TV show *Friends* (Season 5, Episode 4), Phoebe and Joey argue about whether there can be a selfless good deed. Joey says there cannot, so Phoebe decides to prove him wrong. She rakes a neighbour's leaves, allows a bee to sting her and donates money to a charity she dislikes. Each time, her true motive was to advance her own concerns (to prove Joey wrong). In so doing, she proves Joey right.

Ethical theory that matches the moral agent's psychological state

REVISED

Psychological Egoism differs from Ethical Egoism. Psychological Egoism reinterprets our motives so that any apparent altruism is understood as egoism in disguise. We may not even realise that we are acting out of self-interest. Ethical Egoism says that what we ought to do is the same as what we actually do – which is to act according to our own concerns.

> **Prescriptive** – enforcing a rule or method.

Psychological Egoism	Ethical Egoism
We *do* act in our own self-interest, motivated by our own concerns.	We *ought* to act only according to our own concerns and to further our own cause.
A description of reality.	A normative, **prescriptive** theory.
There is no such thing as altruism.	Altruistic-type acts should be avoided unless they are in our own interests.
We are not free to act any other way.	We act wrongly when we act against our own interests.

Concentration on long-term self-interests rather than short-term interests

REVISED

Self-interested actions are not always concerned with immediate gratification. A seemingly selfless act can have a self-interested long-term goal. A business may help someone by giving them a free product, but this provides the organisation with positive advertising and business.

Ayn Rand argued that selfless behaviour is short-sighted, creating a society that treats individuals as disposable, by 'honouring' their self-sacrifice for the benefit of manipulative rulers.

Long-term self-interest means that we can create a society where individuals satisfy their own best interests. You can still help people in need. If you want to, nothing will stop you.

In the TV show *The Good Place* (Season 1), Eleanor wants to learn to be a good person. With Chidi's help, she learns to perform actions that help others. Initially, Eleanor finds these acts frustrating because they interfere with her short-term interests (like learning to fly). However, she learns to focus not on altruism but on her long-term interest, which is to belong in 'The Good Place'.

Revision activity

Watch any episode of *The Good Place* (available on Netflix at time of publishing). Make a chart of the main character's actions in the episode. Have one column that lists that character's short-term interests and one that lists their long-term interests.

Now test yourself   TESTED ☐

1 Give an example of a good deed that appears to be altruistic.
2 What reinterpretation could this act be given to show self-interested motives?
3 Why is Ethical Egoism described as a teleological ethic?

Self-interest as the root cause of every human action even if it appears altruistic

REVISED ☐

Egoism claims that actions that seem altruistic are done out of self-interest. The Golden Rule in Christianity is a good example: 'Do to others as you would have them do to you' is the claim that if you treat others well, they will treat you well when you need it. Altruism is ultimately egoistic.

Existentialism – a philosophical position that says we are free to act without guiding authority.

Nihilism – rejection of moral principles, emphasis on meaninglessness of life.

Anarchism – societal disorder without guidance from law.

Who was Max Stirner?
Max Stirner (1806–1856) was a German philosopher and teacher who influenced the development of **existentialism**, **nihilism** and individual **anarchism**. His most influential work was *The Ego and Its Own* (1844).

Psychological Egoism says that self-interest is the root cause of human action even when it appears to be altruistic.

In contrast, Stirner claimed:
● We think we are acting out of self-interest, but we are not.
● We are slaves to other interests like duty, guilt or conscience.
● We are deceived into thinking it is in our self-interest to obey those interests.

Acts are neither altruistic nor self-interested. Instead, they are controlled by a sense of duty to some other value. For example:

Suzanne Spaak, a wealthy French mother and housewife, put herself at risk by working to hide Jews during the Second World War, particularly the sick and children. She was arrested and killed by the Nazis for her work.

Self-interested motive	Controlling motive
Suzanne wanted to fight against Nazism in France.	Suzanne is controlled by loyalty to France.
She valued ideals such as equality.	Religious moral norms control her.
She was searching for fulfilment.	Responsibility to others controls her.

The root cause is not the self, but obligation. These hidden controls remove our freedom to choose our own best interest. Even when we think we have thrown off these shackles, they remain, ghost-like, behind our motives.

Stirner argued:
1 The ego (**Einzige**) is a slave to obligations.
2 Freedom comes when I recognise my ownness (**Eigenheit**) or authority over myself.
3 Ownness is realised by understanding that our uniqueness (**Einzig**) gives us power to make our own decisions.

> **Revision tip**
>
> Inventing examples of your own can help you grasp the main principles of Stirner's argument.

> **Einzige** – ego.
> **Eigenheit** – ownness.
> **Einzig** – unique.

Rejection of egoism for material gain

REVISED

One obligation we feel is to our physical desires. What is in my self-interest may not even be bound by these desires. My uniqueness gives me power over my physical desires. This means I need not be materialistic to be an egoist.
● How the agent behaves depends upon their own unique nature.
● No one has any obligation to anyone else.
● Each ego operates according to self-interest.
● There is no benefit to an ego to be greedy or anti-social.
● There is benefit to an ego to co-operate with other egos to some extent.

Now test yourself

TESTED

1 What does Stirner mean when he says we are slaves to obligations?
2 Why wouldn't people become greedy if they followed egoism?
3 What does the term Einzige mean?

Union of egoists

REVISED

There is no obligation to other egos, but it is practical to find unprincipled ways of recognising that other unique egos are operating around us. Stirner did not advocate a system of laws. But egos can co-operate to preserve their own identity. He called this the union of egoists. Egos can forge temporary connections with other egos for their own benefit, while remaining independent and self-determining.

> **Typical mistake**
>
> Make sure you can confidently use and define the key words from the text correctly and in context in your essay responses. Many students forget these under pressure of the examination.

Challenges

REVISED

Destruction of a community ethos

Laws benefit the majority and guard against exploitation. Stirner appears to advocate anarchy. There is no obligation to overthrow the state, but he does seem to think it will collapse if egoism is realised. The union of egoists cannot replace this idea of community because it would simply be replacing one set of obligations with another. Ethical Egoism cannot provide solutions to a community when there are inevitable conflicts of interest.

Social injustices could occur as individuals put their own interests first

When all egos pursue their own interests, they come into conflict with others. For example, it is in my self-interest to park my car outside my friend's house when I visit. If someone else comes and parks there, it conflicts with my interests. Everyone serving their own interests leads to quarrelling and conflict. Ethical Egoism gives no fair way of resolving such issues.

A form of bigotry

Moral theories that decree deontological laws are often accused of **bigotry**. In the same way, if we pursue only our own self-interest then it leaves us open to judging other egos with different self-interests than our own. Egoism divides the world into two categories: ourselves and everyone else, the interests of ourselves being more important. But this is an arbitrary divide. It is the same kind of division that racists make when dividing between black and white or sexists dividing men from women and saying it is justified because one is more important than the other.

> **Bigotry** – intolerance of those who hold different ideas.

Apply your knowledge

Three egoists arrive at a car park in their own cars. There is one parking space that is near the exit and all three of them wish to park there. Try to establish what solutions there might be to this dilemma. What kinds of problems do you foresee?

Exam checklist

Can you:
- define what is meant by self-interest and altruism
- give three differences between Psychological and Ethical Egoism
- explain where the two types of egoism converge
- explain the difference between Stirner's egoism and Ethical Egoism in general
- use and define the three German terms for the development from slavery to freedom
- explain why egoism is not materialistic
- define what is meant by the union of egoists
- explain the three challenges to egoism?

Issues for analysis and evaluation

There are six issues for analysis and evaluation listed on the specification as examples of the kinds of AO2 questions you could be asked. Consider the possible conclusions to the question before you establish lines of argument. Develop these lines of argument by giving examples or evidence to demonstrate the points.

Whether morality is what God commands

REVISED

Morality is intrinsically the same as what God commands	Morality is nothing to do with the commands of God	We cannot know if morality is what God commands
The character of God dictates that his commands must be objectively good.	Morality is a human construct; what is good is relative to culture and circumstance.	Some of God's commands are not consistent with our idea of goodness.
Most faiths have the same laws in common. Confusion occurs with humans not God.	Religions conflict over moral laws. They can't all be right, so they may all be wrong.	There is no obvious reason for us to select one religious morality over another.
Without God, morality makes no sense, as there is nothing to be dutiful towards.	The meta-ethical theory of Emotivism says that morality is just an expression of emotion.	If it is, then God appears to command arbitrarily if we use scripture as our evidence.
Adams' modification of the Divine Command (see page 8) shows morality as intrinsically part of God's nature.	There is no evidence to show that morality has any connection with God at all.	The Euthyphro dilemma can be restated and so still stands after Adams' modification.

Whether being a good person is better than just doing good deeds

REVISED

Being a good person is better than doing good deeds	Good deeds are better than being a good person	They are equally important
Good deeds can be used to hide an insincere character and poor intentions.	It is the effects of moral actions that people have to live with.	The two things are intrinsically linked and cannot be separated.
Jesus constantly spoke out against the Pharisees, who followed law for praise.	We would not ask a selfish person to stop a good deed because of weak motives.	A truly good person is going to desire to perform good acts.
Develop virtues first and good deeds will follow naturally.	If we do good deeds, then it will help us to develop a virtuous character.	A virtuous character leads other people, as a good example, via their actions.
Moral excellence is achieved only with practice and is harder than just obeying the law.	Doing good deeds is easier and so more accessible for everyone.	They are two essential strands of morality that are both needed for moral excellence.

Whether Virtue Theory is useful when faced with a moral dilemma

Virtue Theory is useful when faced with a moral dilemma	Virtue Theory is useless when faced with a moral dilemma	Virtue Theory offers some help but is not exclusive
It has experienced a rise in popularity because it is adaptable to modern life.	No instructions are given on what to do when faced with a moral problem.	Sometimes rules can cause more problems, so virtue can guide people when law fails.
It underpins other theories, like Natural Law, and allows reasoned decision-making.	It is impossible to legislate a society that is focused on virtue rather than acts.	Virtue is not a system of law. It works best as a personal ethic alongside a legal system.
As an ancient theory, it is tenacious because it is useable in any culture or time.	The virtues give no method of deciding between two acts that are equally problematic.	Virtues, once developed, might give people the skills to make some challenging decisions.
We need virtue to underpin moral law-making so that laws are reasonable and just.	It can lead to immorality since there is no universal list of standards to apply to all.	A truly virtuous person will never do anything to harm others in society.

The extent to which Ethical Egoism inevitably leads to moral evil

Ethical Egoism will inevitably lead to moral evil	Ethical Egoism does not necessitate moral evil	Ethical Egoism allows moral evil as a possible side effect
People are free to harm others without judgement if it suits their own interests.	Just because people are free to cause harm does not mean that they will.	Deliberate harm is in no one's self-interest, but it could be a by-product.
A union of egoists still offers no obligation to act in a way that protects the weak.	The union of egoists ensures people recognise the freedoms of others.	It is in my self-interest to co-operate with others, but I don't owe them anything.
Egoism is idealistic and assumes that no one will be interested in harming another.	The only moral evil in egoism is neglecting personal interest.	Self-interest motivates all other moral theories; they in turn enslave us. This is evil.
Egoism gives people no reason to act for the good of the many.	Rand says that communities will be fairer if they do act egoistically.	Our current society shows that we are incapable of being consistently co-operative.

The extent to which all moral actions are motivated by self-interest

All moral actions are motivated by self-interest	It is possible to perform an altruistic act	Self-interest as motivation is illusory
People will do things to benefit others only if it makes them feel good.	There are plenty of examples of historical people who put others before themselves.	Moral actions balance self-interest with the interests of others.
We might not do it consciously, but we only do things that we want to do.	Religious and political martyrs have no self-interest served by their own death.	Stirner claims we are mostly bound by obligation and not free anyway (see page 15).
Altruism is just putting aside one self-interest in preference for another self-interest.	Altruism doesn't require the absence of a positive result for the agent as a side effect.	Our apparent self-interest is controlled by a sense of guilt or duty controlling us.
People will reinterpret their values and ideals to suit their self-interest.	Many people hold fast to ideals even when it causes them harm.	The reason we hold fast or reinterpret values is due to external controls.

Whether one of Divine Command Theory, Virtue Theory or Ethical Egoism is superior to the other theories

REVISED

One of the theories is better than the others	All the theories are equally weak	One theory is less practical than any other
Divine Command Theory is the simplest account of morality and the easiest to follow.	All these theories make moral reasoning redundant. Why is X good? Because it is.	There is no reason why what is good for God will have positive outcomes for us.
Virtue Theory is a more holistic ethic that looks deeper than just the act.	All of these theories focus on the well-being or happiness of people and neglect the planet.	Virtue Theory is impossible to legislate for in government.
Ethical Egoism is fairer as it values the individual instead of sacrificing them.	None of these theories gives a practical system by which we can organise society.	There is no way to legislate for Ethical Egoism. There can be no co-ordination of people.
All moral theories are egotistically motivated anyway, so Ethical Egoism is superior.	If all moral theories are motivated by self-interest, then they all fail to be moral.	Divine Command Theory assumes the existence of a God that has yet to be proven.

Specimen exam questions

Sample AO1 questions

1 Outline Aristotle's Virtue Theory. **(AS only)**
2 Compare the ethical theories of Virtue Theory and Ethical Egoism.
3 Examine the challenges levelled at Divine Command Theory.
4 Explain Ethical Egoism with reference to Max Stirner.

Sample AO2 questions

1 Evaluate the view that Virtue Theory is impractical when faced with a moral dilemma.
2 'There is no such thing as a selfless good deed.' Evaluate this view.

> **Revision tip**
>
> Set a timer for five minutes. Write a list of all the ideas you would include in one of the AO1 questions, within that time. Check it against your notes. Gradually reduce your planning time to help you practise speeding up.

> **Revision tip**
>
> Show your understanding of key words that appear in the question, such as 'superior' or 'impractical'. If you show what you understand these words to require, it will help you focus your answer more effectively.

1D Meta-ethical approaches – Naturalism

This meta-ethical theory became popular during the nineteenth century. It is concerned with the meaning of ethical language. It states that the meaning of ethical words like 'good' or 'bad' can be found in the empirical world. This is a kind of **moral realism**, where statements like 'murder is wrong' can have an objective reality.

> **Moral realism** – the meta-ethical view that there exist moral facts.

Objective moral laws exist independently of human beings

`REVISED`

Like Divine Command Theorists, Ethical Naturalists claim that there is an objective standard of good. Naturalists claim 'good' can be:

- known independent of human opinion
- **verified** or **falsified**
- observable
- intrinsic to certain items/actions.

> **Verify** – to check truth or accuracy.
>
> **Falsify** – to demonstrate as false.

Examples of Ethical Naturalist theories are:

Scholar	Theory	Definition of 'good'
Aquinas	Natural Law	The God-given created purpose of an item, observable in nature
Mill	Utilitarianism	Whatever creates maximum happiness, observable in the world
Aristotle	Virtue Ethics	Eudaemonia – observable in society

Moral terms can be understood by analysing the natural world

`REVISED`

Where Ethical Naturalists differ from Divine Command Theorists is that Ethical Naturalists find their evidence for good or bad in the empirical world, while Divine Command Theorists find their evidence through revelation. Ethical Naturalists take a more scientific approach to ethics. Moral statements can be factual in the same way that chemical properties are facts. We use sensory information and apply logical faculties to it to obtain factual truth.

Ethical statements are cognitivist and can be verified or falsified

`REVISED`

Ethical Naturalists treat ethical statements in the same way as any other statement about the natural world. These statements are cognitivist. This means that we can check and then know that the statements contain facts about the world. Naturalists would say this is the most accurate way of doing ethics. It is much more reliable than revelation or intuition.

Cognitive statements	Non-cognitive statements
Objective	Subjective
Can be checked with empirical evidence	Have no method of checking
Factual if true	Not factual
True or false	Not true or false
E.g. Trees absorb carbon dioxide	E.g. 'To thine own self be true'
Murder is wrong (Ethical Naturalists)	Murder is wrong (Emotivists)

Verified moral statements are objective truths and universal

REVISED

Once an ethical statement has been verified as true, this means that it is an objective fact and true regardless of opinion. It can be applied universally to all people regardless of culture or situation. In the case of Mill, the objective truth is that goodness is the same as what makes people happy. For Aquinas, the fact is that goodness is what is consistent with God's created purpose. These facts are true regardless of culture or time.

> **Typical mistake**
>
> You are primarily concerned with the meaning of the words good, bad, right or wrong, not with what the moral laws are. Remember this is meta-ethics, not normative or applied ethics.

Now test yourself

TESTED

1 How can we know the meaning of ethical language?
2 What makes Ethical Naturalism different from Divine Command Theory?
3 What can we do to check the meaning of ethical language?

F.H. Bradley – ethical sentences express propositions

REVISED

> **Who was F.H. Bradley?**
> Francis Herbert Bradley (1846–1924) was an influential British idealist philosopher who attended University College, Oxford and was elected to a fellowship at Merton College, Oxford. His book *Ethical Studies* (1876) is a significant contribution to Ethical Naturalism.

> **Typical mistake**
>
> Bradley is not a typical example of an Ethical Naturalist. He gave a good account of it in his essay 'My Station and Its Duties', but reverted to a more idealist, Hegelian position by the end of the book.

Moral language, such as the words 'good', 'bad', 'right' or 'wrong', rests upon certain **propositions** that can be demonstrated as true or false. These moral judgements are grounded in reality.

Bradley rejected:

● hedonism – pleasure does not lead to self-understanding (Utilitarianism)
● duty for duty's sake – it is a false abstraction (Kantian Ethics).

> **Proposition** – a statement or assertion that expresses a judgement.

He attempted a fusion of the best aspects of each of these approaches. Ethical statements express facts about the world, our position in society and thus our moral duty. To be moral is to live according to our position in society.

Objective features of the world make propositions true or false

REVISED

Human beings are not isolated egos. We are social creatures that co-operate with and impact upon other creatures. We can know what is good or bad by observing objective features of our world, and our place in society. Influenced by Hegel, Bradley thought that self-fulfilment would be achieved through understanding and then satisfying our role in our family and community, to achieve unity with God. This is our moral duty that can be found by observing the empirical world.

> **Revision tip**
>
> To help your understanding of Bradley, think of examples of moral or immoral acts. List all the observable features of this act in its nature and within society.

Meta-ethical statements can be seen in scientific terms

REVISED ☐

We can know our societal role by observation and analysis of the society in which we live. We can observe the destructive nature of some acts and deduce that these acts are wrong. Equally, we can observe constructive acts and deduce that they are right and therefore they are our duty. So, moral statements are cognitivist because they are observable and analysable through reference to the empirical world. Ethics is a branch of scientific investigation.

Moral statement	Observable facts
Murder is wrong	Murder disrupts society. It causes a break in family life. It removes a person from their societal role. Murder causes physical destruction of life. It introduces fear into families and the whole of society.
Giving to charity is good	Giving to charity contributes to society. It builds weak community groups, it is cohesive and binds groups of people together. It enables societal roles to be established.

Now test yourself

TESTED ☐

1 Where can we observe moral facts?
2 What is morally good according to Bradley?
3 How can I know that murder is wrong?

Challenges

REVISED ☐

Hume's Law

In *A Treatise of Human Nature*, David Hume (1711–1776) stated that what we observe in the natural world (facts/'is' statements) gives us a picture of what the world is like, but we cannot infer from these what the world ought to be like.

Premises	Conclusion
Murder is the ending of a life.	Therefore, we ought not to murder.
It is disapproved of by society.	
It is traumatic for both victim and family.	

In this example, there are numerous facts about the world. They are used to conclude what we ought or ought not to do. The error is that there is nothing in the premises that necessitates the conclusion. Hume's Law states that an 'ought' cannot be derived from an 'is'. The ought statement is prescriptive and comes from our feelings about the facts in front of us. It is not a moral fact.

Moore's Naturalistic Fallacy

In *Principia Ethica*, G.E. Moore (1873–1958) claimed that it is an error to define an ethical property in the same way as a natural one. Good, like the colour yellow, is **sui generis**, simple and cannot be broken down into constituent parts for definition. We may define a horse according to its

> **Sui generis** – unique.

four legs, mane and hooves, but we cannot do this by defining goodness as happiness, virtue or what is natural.

Influenced by Hume, he claimed Ethical Naturalists conflate natural and moral properties. For example: a baby is born, I feel happy, so I state that we ought to have babies. Moore says that using a non-moral premise to establish a moral conclusion is an error or fallacy.

The open question argument

A closed question can be settled easily by defining terms, whereas an open question cannot.

Closed question	Open question
● Premise: John is a bachelor.	● Premise: What is natural is good.
● Closed question: Yes, but is he single?	● Open question: Yes, but is it good?

In an open question, the answer cannot be deduced from the premise. Attempts to conflate morality with a natural property will always produce an open question, but a definition should produce a closed question. If good equals natural, then we can always substitute natural for good.

Abortion is not natural.	Abortion is not good.
Taking medicine is not natural.	Taking medicine is not good.
Eating is natural.	Eating is good.
Sickness is natural.	Sickness is good.
What is good is natural.	What is natural is natural.

Evidently, this does not work. We must then ask the open question, 'But is what is natural what is good?'

> **Revision activity**
>
> Put each key word, scholar and key idea for this topic onto a separate small piece of paper. Place in a box and jumble up. Select three random pieces of paper and explain the relationship between them.

> **Apply your knowledge**
>
> 1 Using the example of abortion, homosexuality or immigration, show how Bradley would determine the good thing to do.
> 2 Construct 'is' and 'ought' statements from your examples.

Exam checklist

Can you:
● define Ethical Naturalism
● explain how we can arrive at moral terms
● define and use the terms cognitive, verified, falsified, universal, proposition and realism
● explain who F.H. Bradley was
● explain how he determined what was good
● explain the three objections to Naturalism
● give examples to demonstrate each objection?

1E Meta-ethical approaches – Intuitionism

Objective moral laws exist independently of human beings

REVISED ☐

Intuitionism (**Ethical Non-Naturalism**) became popular at the start of the eighteenth century and has gone in and out of fashion. All Intuitionists claim that there are basic, self-evident, moral facts that cannot be defined with reference to the natural world, but which nonetheless can be known. These facts are **a priori** and not subject to opinion or relative to culture. They exist objectively and apply universally. Well-known advocates of Intuitionism include G.E. Moore, W.D. Ross and H.A. Pritchard.

> **Ethical Non-Naturalism** – another term for Intuitionism.
>
> **A priori** – prior to physical evidence or experience.

Moral truths can be discovered by using our minds in an intuitive way

REVISED ☐

Intuition is:
- an immediate intellectual awareness
- not demonstrable with empirical evidence
- not based on anything rational
- recognition of the self-evident
- different from a belief
- different from a hunch
- adequate justification for action
- understandable
- innate.

A moral intuition will present itself to the mind as true and is unanalysable.

Intuitive ability is innate and the same for all moral agents

REVISED ☐

All humans have the in-built ability to know intuitively the difference between right and wrong. Moore claimed that good, like the colour yellow, is indefinable but meaningful. It is objective, universal and recognisable through intuition. We all recognise these intuitions without need for training or analysis. Moral disagreement is not about the nature of good, it is about the method by which we can bring goodness about.

> **Prima facie** – based on first impression, an initial reason.

Intuition needs a mature mind so not infallible

REVISED ☐

Moral intuitions, like numbers, are true obviously and a priori. The young child may not immediately recognise this, but with maturity it becomes clear and is self-evident. The moral agent requires familiarity with the concept and experience of thinking in this way. So, moral intuitions can be wrong if we are not mature thinkers but, Ross claimed, they do give us a **prima facie** reason to believe them unless there is evidence to the contrary. H.A. Pritchard claimed some of us have a more developed intuition than others.

> **Typical mistake**
>
> Keep one eye on the specification as you revise. An exam question will not ask you for scholars who do not appear on the specification, though they are relevant.

Allows for objective moral values

Intuition can discover basic, foundational truths about morality, prior to any reasoning process. Intuition knows the facts about what is good, then reason works out how to achieve it. Even if an immature mind has misinterpreted its intuition, the standard of goodness still exists independently of the person. What is good is objective and universal in its goodness.

- G.E. Moore argued that we know what is good through intuition; it is then our duty to reason what will bring about the most good (Utilitarianism).
- W.D. Ross argued that we have prima facie duties that are derived from intuition (deontology).

Now test yourself

TESTED

1 What is Ethical Non-Naturalism?
2 How do Non-Naturalists agree with Naturalists?
3 How do they disagree?

Revision activity

Draw a diagram that shows how a person moves from moral knowledge to a moral action according to Intuitionism. Make sure it is labelled with technical vocabulary.

Who was H.A. Pritchard?

Harold Arthur Pritchard (1871–1947) was an English philosopher who studied and worked at Oxford University. He studied mathematics, ancient history and philosophy, and was a professor of moral philosophy, responsible for the paper 'Does Morality Rest on a Mistake?' (1912).

'Ought to do' has no definition

Pritchard agreed with Hume that you cannot derive an ought from an is. He claimed that apprehension of good is immediate and not based on anything else. It is clearly apparent and does not need any supporting evidence from reason or the senses.

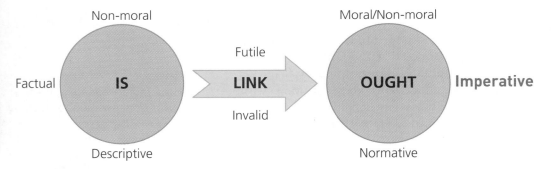

Figure 1.1 The is/ought problem

Even if we could find evidence to prove what good is, there is still no reason that I ought to do it. We are trying to link what is the case with what we ought to do. This link is invalid and trying to prove that it exists will result in frustration.

Imperative – command to act.

Recognise what we 'ought to do' by intuition

- Our feelings of obligation (ought) are immediate intuition.
- They are basic (cannot be reduced to another thing).
- We cannot produce evidence or reasoning for why we should obey them.
- Gathering evidence to support intuition results in deeper uncertainty.
- The best evidence is if we feel the same obligation in the future.
- 'Ought' is deontological not consequentialist.

Two ways of thinking (general and moral)

General thinking	Moral thinking
Reasoning	Intuition
Collects facts	Decides a course to follow
Uses empirical evidence	Self-evident
Does not provide a moral obligation	Recognition of duty
Checks our intuition but doesn't prove it	Not based on reasoning

Intuition helps us decide between apparent conflicting senses of duty or obligation. It helps us understand the greater obligation where reason would fail. Pritchard would not recognise any rational link between the goodness of an action and our sense of obligation – instead our intuition tells us what we ought to do. It establishes specific duties. When we are uncertain about that intuition, our general reasoning can be used to check it, but never as a reason for obeying it. For example:

> I find my best friend's boyfriend is cheating on her. I have a sense of obligation towards my friend to tell her the truth, but also to protect her from harm. Reason would weigh up the consequences of each action but would not tell me what I ought to do. Intuition gives me the answer – I should tell her the truth. However, if I am uncertain, general reasoning can help me to reflect on it, but never to go against my initial intuition.

Typical mistake

Notice that Intuitionists differ slightly on what our intuition is or the way in which it operates. Make sure you know what is specifically different about Pritchard's view.

Now test yourself

1. What is the connection between observable facts and moral obligation?
2. What is the relationship between general thinking and moral thinking?
3. How do I establish a moral rule?

TESTED

Challenges

No proof of moral intuition exists

J.L. Mackie says that there are two ways that we fail to prove the existence of objective intuitive moral knowledge.

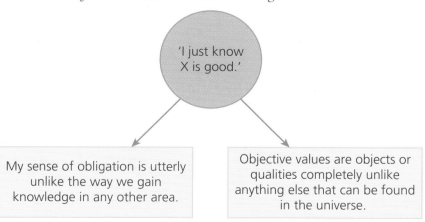

'I just know X is good.'

My sense of obligation is utterly unlike the way we gain knowledge in any other area.

Objective values are objects or qualities completely unlike anything else that can be found in the universe.

Figure 1.2 Mackie's two challenges to Intuitionism

Intuitionism has no basis in empirical knowledge. In any other situation, if I claim something as a fact, I would be expected to produce evidence to support it. Our apparent intuition could simply be psychological conditioning from society.

Intuitive 'truths' can differ widely

If there were an objective truth and we all had the ability to access it, we might expect that we would come to the same conclusions. However, none of the Intuitionists can agree on what is our moral obligation. Some, like Moore, take a consequentialist approach. Others, like Pritchard and Ross, are more deontological. Of these, they cannot agree on any list of duties. It is unclear how we should accurately decide between them.

No obvious way to resolve conflicting intuitions

How do we decide between conflicting intuitions? Intuitionism gives no real guidance on this matter. We are told not to trust reasoning in such matters, so what do we rely upon? Our intuition can even be distorted by unrelated influences, such as the order in which we encounter aspects of a dilemma or the details that are divulged about them. This suggests that such intuitions are not self-evident at all.

Apply your knowledge

In Philippa Foot's Trolley Problem (see page 79), we must decide who to save:
- the five workmen on the left track
- the one workman on the right track.

Do we pull a lever to choose a track? Or do we push a large man off a bridge onto the track to derail the trolley and save all six workmen?

Does it change anything if:
- the large man is the one responsible for the problem
- the one person on the track is someone you love
- the one person on the track has the cure for cancer?

Make a list of the problems you come across when using your intuition rather than reasoning to decide.

Revision tip

The challenges could be more memorable if you draw a chart with the three challenges as headings. Make a list of 3–5 examples of each to illustrate each challenge.

Exam checklist

Can you:
- explain what is meant by Ethical Non-Naturalism
- list the qualities of moral intuition
- give reasons why Intuitionists reject Naturalism
- make use of Hume's Law
- explain why our intuition can sometimes be wrong
- explain Pritchard's support of Hume
- show the difference between moral and general thinking
- examine the three challenges to Intuitionism
- give examples to support your explanations?

1F Meta-ethical approaches – Emotivism

Emotivism originates in the work of the Vienna Circle. This group of philosophers met regularly in the 1920s to discuss philosophy, science and epistemology. Their work on Logical Positivism sought to establish that factually meaningful statements are those that can be verified with empirical evidence.

Theory that believes objective moral laws do not exist

REVISED

The Logical Positivists argued:
- There are only two types of meaningful statement:
  ○ analytic statements – tautologies, mathematical and self-evident statements, because they contain their own definition
  ○ synthetic statements – any statement that can be checked with empirical evidence.
- Moral statements do not express propositions about the empirical world, nor are their properties self-defining; therefore, they are factually meaningless.
- All moral statements are relative and subjective.
- They contain no cognitive properties.

A non-cognitivist theory

REVISED

Non-cognitivism is a form of **irrealism** or **anti-realism**. It says that an ethical statement neither makes any truth claims about the world, nor says anything that can be demonstrated as true or false in any real sense.

> **Moral anti-realism/moral irrealism** – there are no objective moral values.

Moral terms express personal emotional attitudes and not propositions

REVISED

Emotivism claims that an ethical statement only professes a feeling on the part of the speaker and nothing more.
- 'Stealing is wrong' only expresses my feelings about stealing.
- It does not make any truth claim about stealing.
- The claim cannot be evidenced.
- If I felt differently about stealing, then my claim about it would be different.
- A factual claim would remain the same whether I liked it or not.

Ethical terms are just expressions of personal approval or disapproval

REVISED

A moral claim like 'stealing is wrong' is only an emotional expression and not even a statement of belief. Giving reasons to support my statement is just giving examples of my feelings, not logical support. I am just announcing how I feel. In a pantomime, the hero enters the stage and we cheer, the villain appears and we boo or hiss. 'Euthanasia is good' is no more meaningful than me saying 'Euthanasia, hurrah!' Condemning the possession and use of nuclear arms is saying 'Nuclear arms, boo!'

Explains why people disagree about morality

REVISED

C.L. Stevenson explains moral disagreements by differentiating between beliefs and attitudes.

Disagreements in belief (non-moral)	Disagreements in attitude (moral)
Belief propositions concern facts that are believed to be true.	Attitudes concern desires or feelings. They are psychological states.
Conflicting belief statements cannot simultaneously be true.	Conflicting attitudes concern what individuals favour or prefer.

Attitudes and beliefs affect each other, and both are involved in moral debate, but ultimately, disagreements about morality are disagreements in attitude. However, you cannot prove attitudes, so a moral argument is a challenge to shout the loudest feeling. Moral statements attempt to persuade someone to change their attitude.

> **Revision activity**
>
> Choose an example from one of the applied ethics sections of the specification. List three beliefs and three attitudes that might be associated with the debate.

Now test yourself

TESTED

1 What does non-cognitivism mean?
2 Why is Emotivism sometimes known as the 'boo'/'hurrah' theory?
3 How does Stevenson explain moral disagreements?

Ethical statements are neither verifiable nor analytic

REVISED

A.J. Ayer agreed with the Vienna Circle that moral statements are neither analytic nor synthetic. A statement such as 'stealing is wrong' contains no more information than if I said 'stealing!' I can consider the facts of stealing, but it is not possible to analyse the ethical aspect of the statement. The idea of rightness or wrongness is a **pseudo-concept**. It is no different than if I said 'stealing' with a strange look of horror on my face. The look on my face or the size and shape of the exclamation mark attached to the word offer us no analysable content.

> **Pseudo-concept** – a false concept.

> **Who was A.J. Ayer?**
> Alfred Jules Ayer (Freddie) (1910–1989) was a Logical Positivist who admired the work of the Vienna Circle. He was not a member but did visit. He was educated at Eton, Oxford and Vienna and wrote *Language, Truth and Logic* (1936).

> **Revision activity**
>
> Create a chart of the different meta-ethical scholars you have studied to help you remember and differentiate between them. Include their names, a picture, the theory they represent and a bullet point list of the main principles.

Made to express joy or pain

Ayer identified four types of ethical statements:

Four kinds of ethical statement	Category of study
Propositions that define ethical terms	Meta-ethics – the only ethical philosophy according to Ayer
Propositions that describe moral experience	Descriptive ethics – belongs with psychology or sociology
Exhortations of virtue	Normative ethics – does not belong to any category of philosophy or science (emotional statements)
Ethical judgement	Applied ethics – does not belong to any category of philosophy or science (emotional statements)

Ethical judgements are **symbols**. The word 'wrong' or 'right' is a symbol within a sentence that represents the feeling or sensation I get when I think about a particular issue. Such statements have no objective validity. They express joy or pain and so relate to internal sensations rather than to anything objective in the external/empirical world.

> **Symbol** – a word that represents something else (a feeling or sensation).

Expressed to be persuasive

If I make the statement 'Homosexuality is wrong', I also seek to persuade you to feel the same way as me. I can choose different words to make the strength of the statement more urgent (much like I might add more exclamation marks or write in capital letters). The reaction from others is, at best, evidence of how strongly the sensations are felt.

Emotivism is not subjectivism

Ayer claimed that Emotivism was different from subjectivism.

Subjectivism	Emotivism
Ethical statements are expressions of emotion.	Ethical statements are expressions of emotion.
They are propositions about a person's emotional state.	They are emotional utterances.
Such statements can be verifiable.	Such statements contain no facts about the self.

Now test yourself

1 Which kinds of ethical statements are true philosophy according to Ayer?
2 Which did he dismiss as meaningless?
3 Give an example of an ethical statement for each of Ayer's four categories.
4 Give two reasons why Emotivism is not subjectivism.

Challenges

No basic moral principles can be established

Emotivism is too reductionist and gives no basis by which we can establish any moral principles. Even the most self-serving normative ethical position that will be covered in this guide has a basis for an ethical principle or code of some kind.

An egoist would promote the saving of life in as far as it benefits themselves. The relativist would promote saving life provided it produced a result that could be called 'good', like happiness or love. However, Emotivism says that debating this is meaningless because it is the same as saying 'Saving life!' Emotivism is useless in any practical sense.

Ethical debate becomes a pointless activity

Ethical debate is reduced to nothing more than a shouting match, with the winner being the one who can shout the loudest or contort the most expressive face. Surely ethical discussion is more than this? Moral debate is usually about what constitutes a good action and how best to achieve it. Under Emotivism, all we are doing is shouting our feelings into an abyss. We cannot prove or disprove anything that is said, and the reaction relates to nothing empirical.

There is no universal agreement that some actions are wrong

If Emotivism is correct, all normative theories are mistaken and there can be no human rights or acts that are demonstrably wrong. This is so reductionist that it is useless for ordinary life. Emotivism has no practical use at all. Rape and murder are reduced to something that I have unpleasant feelings about but cannot be said to be objectively wrong and we cannot have a meaningful discussion about it.

Typical mistake

Emotivism is a meta-ethical theory and so its job is not to make normative pronouncements on ethical behaviour. It does not have to be practical to be correct, so the above challenge is insufficient to make Emotivism redundant on its own.

Apply your knowledge

1 List ten normative statements that ordinarily have a consensus, e.g. 'Murder is wrong'.
2 Which of these statements are concerning if they are reduced to emotional utterances?
3 Why is this the case?
4 Look back at Naturalism and Intuitionism. Do either of these theories solve the problems you have just raised?

Exam checklist

Can you:
- explain the difference between a cognitivist and non-cognitivist theory
- explain the influence of the Logical Positivists
- show the difference between a moral term and a proposition
- exemplify what moral terms are
- explain what moral disagreements are
- demonstrate Ayer's development of Emotivism
- explain how it is different from subjectivism
- state the three main challenges to Emotivism
- develop examples to illustrate each point?

Issues for analysis and evaluation

There are six issues for analysis and evaluation listed on the specification as examples of the kinds of AO2 questions you could be asked. Consider the possible conclusions to the question before you establish lines of argument. Develop these lines of argument by giving examples or evidence to demonstrate the points.

Whether ethical and non-ethical statements are the same

REVISED

Ethical and non-ethical statements are identical	Ethical and non-ethical statements are distinct	There are some similarities between the two
There is unmistakable evidence in the world to support moral statements.	Neither obligation nor objective values are like anything else in the universe.	Ethical statements are based in the practical world but cannot prove obligation.
Empirical evidence showing the consequences of good and bad actions is available to all.	Moral statements are interpretive and so cannot be universally understandable.	Ethical statements are pragmatic. They communicate useful behaviour.
We get information about acts in the same way whether they are ethical or not.	We get information about moral actions through scripture not nature.	Ethical statements are formulated through pleasant and unpleasant experiences.
Ethical statements affect worldly action and so should be assessed empirically.	Ethical statements just express how people feel, not objective facts about the world.	Our experience of the world influences whether we judge an act as good or bad.

The extent to which ethical statements are not objective

REVISED

Ethical statements are completely subjective	Ethical statements are always based on objective truths	Some ethical statements contain objective truth
Ethical statements mean different things to different people.	How I interpret ethical statements and their objective reality may be different things.	Not all moral statements are interpreted differently. Some are universally agreed upon.
There is no way of ensuring that ethical statements are objectively true.	The best way of ensuring that an ethical statement is true is to look to revelation.	Some statements have stood the test of time and thus indicate objective values.
An ethical command prescribes behaviour and cannot be assessed for truth.	A command is based upon evidence that can be assessed scientifically.	A command may be subjective, but its basis is empirically evident.
Individual intuition clearly tells people different things about right and wrong.	We can make mistakes if our intuition is underdeveloped, but the facts are still objective.	There is a universal consensus over some moral issues. This demonstrates their truth.

Whether moral terms are intuitive

Moral terms are intuitive	Moral terms require rational support, not intuition	Moral terms are intuitive but need rational support
We cannot prove what is good and bad, we just know.	Intuition is very unreliable, and agents could claim any statement as intuitively true.	We have an instinctive reaction to moral issues but a responsibility to check it.
It is universal that people have a gut reaction to certain moral issues. We should trust it.	Freud would argue that this 'gut reaction' is unconscious programming by society.	We shouldn't trust a gut reaction on its own – that would be immoral.
It is more valuable to trust our intuition because it is an honest moral reaction.	We have a responsibility to check 'truths' with reason because they affect others.	Intuition is like faith – it needs support from reason to know it is true.
All cultures share this sense of duty that we feel when confronted with moral issues.	If intuition were universally accurate, we would not have relative moral systems.	Intuition needs reason so that we can know how to act. They support each other.

The extent to which moral terms are just expressions of our emotions

Moral terms are purely emotional utterances	Moral terms cannot be reduced to feelings	Moral terms are linked to emotion and other things too
This explains why we differ so widely on what we perceive is 'moral' or not.	This makes it impossible to decide what we ought to do. No one is right or wrong.	It is possible for us to have an emotional reaction to an objective truth.
Moral terms cannot be verified or falsified and so are nothing more than emotion.	This is unnecessarily reductionist. It does not reflect the complexity of experience.	Objective facts, emotion and intuition may all be factors in moral decision-making.
Moral terms do nothing to explain what is meant by 'good', 'bad', 'right' or 'wrong'.	Moral terms refer to an observable human experience in the world.	We respond emotionally to events in the world. To call this meaningless is too limiting.
Kant argues that we cannot trust empirical data to provide moral certainty.	This would make moral statements useless and impractical.	Ethical statements also link to pragmatism, consequences and cultural expectations.

Whether one of Naturalism, Intuitionism or Emotivism is superior to the other theories

Naturalism is the superior theory	Intuitionism is the superior theory	Emotivism is the superior theory
It gives practical instruction regarding moral behaviour that can be enforced.	It reflects the reality of how we make moral judgements.	It is the most logical possibility when it comes to analysing statements and their meaning.
It gives us certainty and security that the other theories lack.	It provides certainty and autonomy. We are not bound, we sense for ourselves.	It provides the uncomfortable truth about what moral statements are.
Bradley gives us the most scientific and so most attractive theory.	It blends objectivity with human experience to enable us to find moral facts.	Ayer gives us the most scientific account of what is occurring in moral statements.
It provides a basis for building normative systems that can then be checked for accuracy.	It helps to preserve the difference between moral and non-moral statements.	It does not require us to have faith that moral statements are true.

The extent to which the different meta-ethical theories encourage moral debate

REVISED

Meta-ethical theories encourage moral debate	Meta-ethics makes moral debate impossible	Moral debate is dependent on a criterion of meaning
They allow us to consider the assumptions we make about what is good or bad.	It is impossible to move forward in terms of ethical analysis if we are just emoting.	It is vital for consistency that we all agree on a common usage of ethical language.
Naturalism encourages us to discuss our understanding of natural facts.	Emotivism prevents more than discussion of the facts; no judgement can be reached.	Even Intuitionism makes it difficult to debate because we have no common definitions.
The real debate to be had is regarding which meta-ethical theory is correct.	Divine command prevents us from arguing with a moral pronouncement at all.	Naturalism gives us something concrete we can debate about, unlike other theories.
Stevenson's Emotivism encourages debate as moral exhortations are persuasive.	Logical Positivists would say that all such debate is meaningless.	We need clarity in debate. Defining terms through meta-ethics is necessary.

Specimen exam questions

Sample AO1 questions

1 Compare the meta-ethical approaches of Naturalism and Intuitionism.
2 Examine the meta-ethical approach of Emotivism with reference to A.J. Ayer.
3 Explain the challenges to Ethical Naturalism.
4 Compare the work of H.A. Pritchard to that of A.J. Ayer.
5 Examine the cognitivist meta-ethical theory of Ethical Naturalism.

Revision tip

In an AO2 question on meta-ethics, you will not be asked to 'apply'. (This is a trigger word for normative application to ethical problems.)

Sample AO2 questions

1 Evaluate the view that there is no evidence to prove that moral intuition exists.
2 'Meta-ethical theories add nothing useful to ethical debate.' Evaluate this view.

Revision tip

Make sure that you can refer to scholars when weighing up an AO2 question. These don't have to be restricted to named scholars from the specification.

Theme 2 Deontological ethics

There are many **normative** ethical theories that can be described as deontological. You will need to focus on Natural Law as a deontological theory, considering **Thomism**, as well as more modern developments. A deontological ethic focuses on the action itself rather than the goal or the consequences of it. Natural Law considers the correct action to be a duty for all people universally, regardless of the situation.

> **Normative ethics** – ethical systems or rules that govern behaviour.
>
> **Thomism** – the theology of St Thomas Aquinas.
>
> **Natural Theology** – knowledge about God derived from observation of the **empirical** world.
>
> **Empirical** – physical, sensory information.

2A St Thomas Aquinas' Natural Law – laws and precepts as the basis of morality

> **Typical mistake**
>
> Don't forget to define technical vocabulary within your essay. It is vital to show the examiner that you understand Aquinas' approach by explaining what terms like Natural Theology are.

Who was St Thomas Aquinas?
St Thomas Aquinas (1225–1274) was an Italian Dominican friar, Catholic priest and Doctor of the Church. He valued both revelation through scripture and the use of Aristotelian reasoning. As the father of **Natural Theology**, his methods have become part of Roman Catholic doctrine. His major works include *Summa Theologiae* and *Summa Contra Gentiles*.

Aquinas was writing in the Middle Ages from a Christian perspective. He felt that it was possible for us to know God's will, in part, through scripture. However, humans have been given the divine gift of reason, by God at creation. We can use this to discover what is naturally right.

Aquinas' four levels of law

REVISED

According to Aquinas, there are four levels of law that govern God's creation.

The laws exist in a hierarchy. Eternal Law is the foundation of all of God's creation and so nothing can challenge it. The laws found in scripture (Divine Law) are all achievable because they conform to God's created order; they serve as a moral reminder for humans. A Natural Law must conform to God's Eternal and Divine Laws but can be known purely through application of reason. Any Human Law that breaks a Natural or Divine Law is wrong.

Now test yourself

TESTED

1 What is meant by the term Natural Theology?
2 How did Aquinas think we can establish moral laws?
3 What does deontological mean?
4 What is the role of scripture in Natural Law?

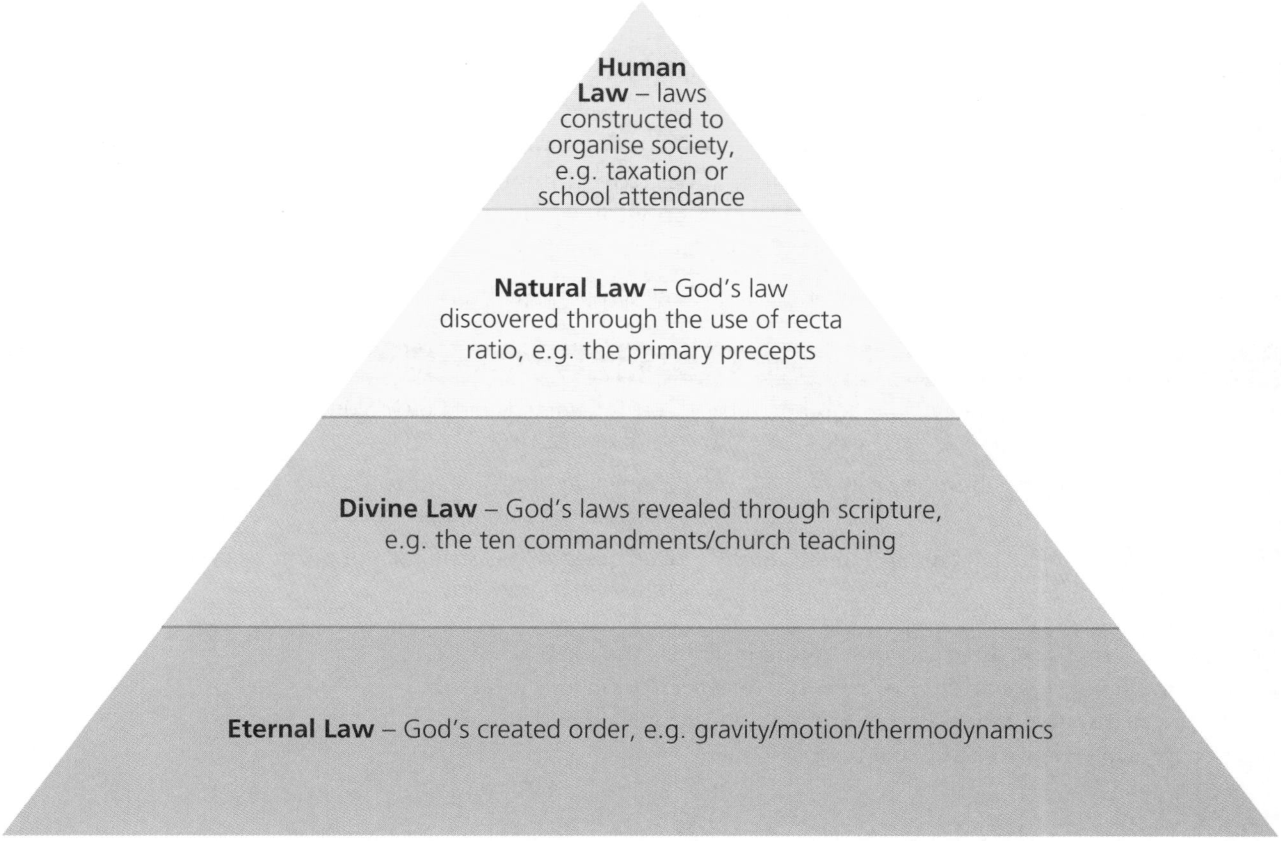
Human Law – laws constructed to organise society, e.g. taxation or school attendance
Natural Law – God's law discovered through the use of recta ratio, e.g. the primary precepts
Divine Law – God's laws revealed through scripture, e.g. the ten commandments/church teaching
Eternal Law – God's created order, e.g. gravity/motion/thermodynamics

Figure 2.1 Aquinas' four levels of law

Natural Law derived from rational thought

REVISED

Aquinas claimed that God gave us reason, or **recta ratio**, at creation when he made us in his image. Natural Law is derived through right reason, by looking at the empirical world and observing God's created purpose for all things. We can use reason to identify our own created purpose, and then choose to follow it.

Based on a belief in a divine creator

REVISED

Aquinas had already established the existence of God in his **demonstratio**. He accepts that there is one God who is the creator of all things. Scripture tells us that everything he created is good.

- Through observation of the empirical world and consideration of God's creative purpose, we can discern the good.
  - For example, an acorn is created to become an oak tree. If it does so, then it is a good acorn – it has served its created purpose.
- The highest good for humanity is the rational understanding of God's final purpose for all of creation (the Beatific Vision).
- God's final purpose for humans is to achieve **fellowship** with him by doing good and avoiding evil.
- This is universal for all of humanity.
- Fellowship with God leads to eternal life with God in heaven.

Recta ratio – Latin, meaning right reasoning; this is our conscience, or reason, making right decisions.

Demonstratio – Latin, meaning demonstration or proof; this refers to Aquinas' five ways to prove the existence of God.

Fellowship – companionship or union.

Natural Law as a form of moral absolutism and a theory which has both deontological and teleological aspects

Aquinas claimed that human beings had a natural desire to aim for the good and that we only fail to do this when we reason wrongly. This means that when a moral rule is established, it is our duty to obey.

Hence, Natural Law shows both deontological and teleological qualities:

Natural Law is deontological (duty-based)	Natural Law is teleological (goal-centred)
It is a universal duty to obey a rule established by reason.	A rule is discovered by looking at the purpose of an item or act.
God created a universal human nature.	Empirical observation is used to establish the purpose/goal of an item or act.
Rules do not change according to the situation or consequences.	God created humans for the purpose of achieving fellowship with him.

For example, empirical observation shows that sex has the purpose of procreation. Thus, it is our duty to have sex for procreation and it is evil to have sex in any way that prevents procreation (for instance, through using contraception or homosexual sex).

The five primary precepts as derived from rational thought and based on the premise of doing good and avoiding evil

Aquinas used recta ratio to establish five primary precepts. These are absolute and should not be violated.
1 **P**reserve innocent life
2 **O**rder society
3 **W**orship God
4 **E**ducate
5 **R**eproduce

These precepts help us to achieve our created purpose of fellowship with God, by doing good and avoiding evil.

Revision tip

You can remember the five primary precepts using the acronym **POWER**.

Now test yourself

Give three ways in which Natural Law is dependent upon the existence of God.

The secondary precepts which derive from the primary precepts

Secondary precepts are established not as a strict set of deontological rules but as direction to explain how to uphold the primary precepts. The secondary precepts are more situation-dependent. They may be broken, if doing so helps to uphold the absolute primary precepts.

In *Les Misérables*, Jean Valjean steals a loaf of bread to feed his starving niece. This is against the secondary precept 'Do not steal'. However, if his niece will die if he doesn't steal the food, he is preserving innocent life by stealing. In this instance, reason may say that he also upholds order by stealing the bread and nurturing his family.

Primary precept	Secondary precepts (examples)
Preserve innocent life	Do not murder
	Do not abort
	Do not euthanise
	Do administer CPR if someone is dying
	Do give medical treatment to preserve life
Order society	Do not steal
	Do not lie
	Monogamous marriage only
	Sex is permitted only between married couples
	Nurture your family

Now test yourself

1 List the five primary precepts.
2 Define recta ratio.
3 How does recta ratio fit into the primary precepts?

TESTED ☐

Revision activity

Try to work out five secondary precepts that can be derived from each of the primary precepts.

The importance of keeping the precepts in order to establish a right relationship with God and gain eternal life with God in heaven

REVISED ☐

- Reason is given as a gift by God to humanity.
- It is what marks us as different from the rest of creation.
- Humans were created by God for fellowship with him.
- We all desire fellowship with God.
- Wrong application of reason is a mistake, not deliberate.
- The fall of Adam and Eve distanced us from him through poor reasoning.
- If we apply right reason to the empirical world, we can establish right moral behaviour.
- The precepts are formulated through right reason.
- If we follow the precepts, we will re-establish fellowship with God.
- Fellowship with God means we will gain eternal life in heaven with him.

Typical mistake

Many students know each of the parts of Aquinas' Natural Law but are unclear about how it all fits together. Make sure you know the relationship between the four levels of law, reason, God and the precepts.

Apply your knowledge

A mad axe murderer is at your door, asking whether your best friend is in the house. He helpfully tells you he wants to torture and kill her. Your best friend is hiding in your spare room. Use the precepts to work out what Natural Law would tell you to do.

Exam checklist

Can you:
- define the following terms: deontological, teleological, recta ratio, fellowship, absolutism, Natural Theology, empiricism
- describe the four levels of law
- list the five primary precepts
- give examples of secondary precepts
- explain the role of reason in Natural Law
- describe the purpose of humanity according to Aquinas
- explain the role of God in Natural Law?

2B Aquinas' Natural Law – the role of virtues and goods in supporting moral behaviour

The need for humans to be more God-like by developing the three revealed virtues and four cardinal virtues

REVISED

Aquinas used a combination of Aristotelian reasoning and scripture to establish two lists of human qualities that we should strive towards.

Revealed virtues	Virtues that cannot be established through reason but are shown to us in scripture – 1 Corinthians 13:13
Faith	Trust in God
Hope	Wish or desire for the future (fellowship with God in heaven)
Love	Agape/charity – altruistic concern for other people

Cardinal virtues	Virtues that can only be established through reason alone
Temperance	Moderation/self-control
Prudence	Wisdom/the ability to judge between actions
Fortitude	Courage/strength of character/confronting fear
Justice	Fair behaviour/treatment of others

If we have perfected our **virtues** through practice, we will become more like God and will have the personal qualities necessary to make correct moral decisions, rather than giving in to temptation and making bad choices.

Virtues – personal qualities, not specific actions or consequences.

Aquinas' definition of different types of acts

REVISED

Aquinas noticed that there is more to an action than simply behaviour. Our intentions are vital in moral decision-making. I can help an old lady across the road, but the action should be judged differently depending on why I do it. I might wish to keep her safe, or I might intend that she be hit by the next oncoming bus! Consequently, Aquinas identified two kinds of action:

Internal/interior acts	External/exterior acts
Our intention – what our aim is when we perform an action.	The act itself – the physical behaviour that we perform.

Both interior and exterior acts must be good for my action to be judged as good. A virtuous person will have good internal acts such as compassion and helpfulness, so perfecting the virtues is vital to ensure that both kinds of acts are good.

Double effect

It is worth mentioning **double effect** here. There are some circumstances where it seems that one act might bring about two possible effects. A good example is that of abortion.

Marie has an **ectopic pregnancy**. If untreated, both mother and baby will die. The primary precept of preserving life forbids abortion, yet we must preserve Marie's life too. If the doctor removes the affected fallopian tube, with the interior act of saving Marie's life, her act is a good one. She is judged on the intended effect, not the second effect (the death of the foetus). This applies despite the doctor's foreknowledge of the second effect, provided she didn't intend it. (Note: It is not acceptable to remove the foetus to preserve the tube, as this involves the interior act of abortion.)

Double effect – literally, two effects; an aspect of Natural Law that allows us to judge intentions over actions.

Ectopic pregnancy – a fertilised egg attaches and develops in the fallopian tube instead of the womb.

Typical mistake

Students often explain double effect without having dealt with any other aspect of Natural Law. It makes sense only once you have established the precepts and the acts.

Now test yourself

TESTED ☐

1 List the revealed virtues.
2 How are the cardinal virtues established?
3 Identify possible interior or exterior acts in the following scenarios:
   a a woman who steals bread to feed her child
   b a man who shoots and kills an intruder who breaks into his home
   c a doctor who gives a large dose of painkiller to a suffering patient.

Revision tip

The revealed virtues are famously represented by the three graces. Consider how you would depict each virtue (e.g. justice could be weighing scales) to help you remember them.

Aquinas' definition of different types of goods

REVISED ☐

Real good	Apparent good
An action that is good, independent of individual opinion. Right reason will establish a real good with the help of the virtues. This will help a human achieve their purpose of fellowship with God.	A sin. An action that seems good if we lack virtue and have reasoned wrongly. These mistakes will lead people away from their purpose of fellowship with God.

Aquinas understood that sometimes we sin. But he had a positive view of humanity and believed that we all desire to aim towards God and to do good. We often find ourselves going down the wrong path, not because we desire evil but due to wrong reasoning, we believe something is good when it is not.

Typical mistake

Students often muddle acts and goods. You must know the difference between the two terms.

Now test yourself

According to Natural Law, arrange the following actions into real and apparent goods:

a abortion
b sex with a girlfriend
c administering CPR
d sex within marriage
e euthanasia
f telling the truth
g going to church
h attending school
i using birth control
j murder.

Revision activity

Create a flow diagram that shows the connections between the various aspects of Natural Law. Consider how the virtues might help someone who is trying to follow the precepts. Think about how the good and the acts might relate to recta ratio from the previous section.

Apply your knowledge

You are a doctor and you have a sick patient who is begging to be allowed to die. They are in pain and have a life-limiting condition, but they are not about to die imminently. How would the virtues help you, the doctor? How might they help your patient?

Exam checklist

Can you:
- define the following terms: virtue, real good, apparent good, interior act, exterior act
- give examples of each of the terms above
- provide a synonym for each of the virtues: faith, hope, love, prudence, temperance, justice and fortitude
- explain how each of the elements of Natural Law relate to each other?

2C Aquinas' Natural Law – application of the theory

The application of Aquinas' Natural Law to abortion

REVISED

Abortion is the medical procedure of ending a pregnancy so that it does not result in the birth of a baby. Sometimes it is called a termination. There are several ways of doing this:
- taking medicine (a morning-after pill)
- having a surgical procedure (vacuum aspiration or D&E).

The method chosen will depend on how far along the pregnancy has progressed. In UK law, pregnancy may be terminated before 24 weeks, except in the case of foetal abnormality.

What does scripture/Divine Law teach?

There is no reference to abortion in the Bible. However, there are many verses that can be interpreted as having relevance to the debate:

> 'Parents shall not be put to death for their children, nor shall children be put to death for their parents; only for their own crimes may persons be put to death.'
>
> Deuteronomy 24:16 (NRSV)
>
> 'Before I formed you in the womb I knew you,
> and before you were born I consecrated you;
> I appointed you a prophet to the nations.'
>
> Jeremiah 1:5 (NRSV)
>
> 'Sons are indeed a heritage from the Lord,
> the fruit of the womb a reward.'
>
> Psalm 127:3 (NRSV)

Church teaching varies according to denomination; however, in general, there is a strong tendency to reject abortion or allow it only in very exceptional cases. Human life is considered **sacred**, and it is for God alone to decide when it should end.

Sacred – holy, dedicated to God.

What would Aquinas say?

Any action must be in accordance with recta ratio and thus the primary precepts. These are absolute and can sometimes be confirmed through Divine Law but will never contradict it. Once the law has been established, it is our duty to obey it so that we can achieve our God-given purpose.

Sky is 16. She is 12 weeks pregnant. She is unmarried, and her boyfriend is unable to support her. Her parents will disown her if they find out that she is pregnant.

Revision tip

Learn these worked examples, or other examples that you have prepared beforehand. This will be of significant help in the examination when you are under pressure.

WJEC and Eduqas A level Religious Studies Religion and Ethics

43

Cardinal virtues:
Justice – she won't punish the child for parental mistakes.
Prudence – she will reason wisely.
Fortitude – she will be courageous when it gets difficult.

Should Sky have an abortion?

Revealed virtues:
Love – she will show care and concern to the child.

Telos/aim:
to do good and avoid evil to achieve fellowship with God.

Recta ratio (right reason) must be applied:

Primary precept
Preserve life
Reproduce

Secondary precept
Do not abort

— **Real good!**

An abortion would be **a sin/apparent good**. She must **intend** to keep the baby, not just fail in any attempt to abort.

Figure 2.2 The application of Natural Law to the ethical issue of abortion

In this example, Sky has a duty to preserve the life of the unborn child and to reproduce. As a deontological theory, Natural Law gives her the responsibility to perform these acts, not the right to choose whether she does. This kind of argument is **pro-life** rather than **pro-choice**.

Pro-life – in opposition to actions that end a human life.

Pro-choice – in support of the right of a woman to choose whether she has a child.

Now test yourself

TESTED

1 Which aspects of Natural Law are not mentioned in the example above?
2 Could you apply any of them to this example?

The application of Aquinas' Natural Law to voluntary euthanasia

REVISED

- **Voluntary euthanasia** is when a person has asked to be killed to ease their suffering (sometimes called 'mercy killing').
- It contrasts with **involuntary euthanasia** or **non-voluntary euthanasia**.
- This is different from murder as the person being killed is usually terminally ill or requires burdensome medical treatment to stay alive.
- It is different from suicide because it requires the assistance of another person when the patient cannot carry out the act themselves.
- It can include giving lethal medication (active euthanasia – where the individual actively brings about death).
- It can be the refusal of medical treatment, food or drink (passive euthanasia – where an individual exercises their legal right to refuse treatment).
- UK law does not allow active voluntary euthanasia.

Voluntary euthanasia – 'gentle, easy death' or mercy killing, requested by the patient as a solution to extreme physical suffering.

Involuntary euthanasia – killing as a solution to extreme physical suffering that has been specifically rejected by the patient at an earlier stage.

Non-voluntary euthanasia – mercy killing that has not been addressed specifically by the patient, e.g. in the case of a small child or someone with severe mental disabilities.

What does scripture/Divine Law teach?

Scripture does not directly forbid voluntary euthanasia. However, there are plenty of teachings that may apply to this issue. Scripture condemns murder and supports the sanctity of life. The New Testament recounts Jesus' refusal of a narcotic substance to ease his pain when dying. In the Old Testament, a man falsely claims to have killed Saul at his own request when he was mortally wounded in battle. David, believing the account, condemns the man's actions.

'You shall not murder.'

Exodus 20:13 (NRSV)

'And they offered him wine mixed with myrrh; but he did not take it.'

Mark 15:23 (NRSV)

'David said to him, "Your blood be on your head; for your own mouth has testified against you, saying, 'I have killed the Lord's anointed'."'

2 Samuel 1:16 (NRSV)

Church teaching generally condemns euthanasia. In the Roman Catholic Church, it is specifically condemned in various papal statements, including those by Pope Francis.

What would Aquinas say?

Our actions must be in accordance with right reasoning. By looking at the primary precepts, we should be able to apply reason to establish what to do. Aquinas' precepts seem to favour quantity of life rather than the quality of life that is being experienced. They also treat life as a duty or responsibility rather than an optional right.

Tyler has terminal lung cancer. He is midway through a second round of chemotherapy, which doctors think will give him another six months of life. Tyler has decided that he has had enough suffering and would like to stop the treatment. He has asked a doctor to help him to die quickly and painlessly.

Apply your knowledge

Try to apply the principles of Natural Law to the following situations to decide what is acceptable:

1 A young man is on dialysis with stage 5 diabetes. His only hope is a kidney transplant. He refuses further treatment.
2 An elderly woman near the end of her life wishes for help to die.
3 A middle-aged woman with early onset Alzheimer's, but otherwise healthy, wants to end her life, but needs help.

Revision activity

Construct a flow chart to show the decision-making process for someone following Natural Law. This may help you keep track of all the important elements.

Tyler			Tyler's doctor		
Useful virtues:	**Hope** – for eternal life in heaven with God		Useful virtues:	**Love** – compassion for his patient	
	Faith – trust in God's will			**Prudence** – wise decision-making, right reasoning	
	Fortitude – courage to face what is coming			**Temperance** – moderate behaviour, avoiding extremes	

Right reason should be applied so that **good may be done and evil avoided** in line with God's purpose (the highest good).

Primary precepts	Secondary precepts
Preserve life	Do not kill, do not euthanise, give medical treatment to preserve life
Worship God	Follow God's Divine Law
Order society	Follow Human Law, do not lie

The **apparent good** is to ease Tyler's suffering since he desires this. However, this is a sin. Right reason shows that the **real good** is to preserve life in accordance with the primary precepts and God's authority.

The law of double effect

There might be a way that Tyler's doctor can help. If Tyler is in so much pain that the safe dose of painkillers or anaesthetic is not helping him, the doctor can administer a stronger dose to make him comfortable. The double effects here are:

- easing Tyler's pain
- killing him with a dangerously high dose.

The doctor's interior act is to ease Tyler's pain. In this case, his act is morally justified. If he performed the act with the intention of killing Tyler, it would be a sin.

Typical mistake

In an essay, many students get distracted by their own beliefs about such controversial topics. Remember that the examiner cannot award marks for your opinion, even in an AO2 question. You need to show the way that Natural Law works and, in an AO2 question, weigh up how effective the theory is.

Now test yourself
TESTED

1 Define voluntary euthanasia.
2 Which primary precepts are most useful when deciding about euthanasia?
3 What would Aquinas call the apparent good of euthanasia?

Exam checklist

Can you:
- define the following terms: abortion, voluntary euthanasia
- state a brief scenario to work with for each moral issue
- apply the virtues to your worked example
- list the primary precepts that are most relevant to your example
- show how to arrive at secondary precepts based on the primary precepts
- use the terms real good, apparent good, interior act, exterior act, recta ratio and final purpose effectively in your response
- refer to Bible references to support your response?

Issues for analysis and evaluation

There are six issues for analysis and evaluation listed on the specification as examples of the kinds of AO2 questions you could be asked. Consider the possible conclusions to the question before you establish lines of argument. Develop these lines of argument by giving examples or evidence to demonstrate the points.

The degree to which Human Law should be influenced by Aquinas' Natural Law

REVISED

Human Law should be based purely upon Natural Law	Human Law should not be based upon Natural Law	Natural Law has something to offer Human Law
Human Law upholds Natural Law and reflects the primary precept of 'order society'.	We live in a secular society, so our laws should not be influenced by religion.	The primary precept 'order society' supports obedience to Human Law.
Human Law is just a practical expression of Natural Law.	Human Law is a practical response to problems of the day, not a set of moral rules.	Natural Law has stood the test of time. It is worth listening to its suggestions.
Natural Law is established via the God-given gift of right reason.	Not everyone believes in God, so it is inappropriate to govern them with religious laws.	This Roman Catholic doctrine should be considered as there are many Catholics in society.
Natural Law is ordained by God. It can be trusted to make correct decisions.	Human Law should respond to today's needs, not outdated laws.	Both types of law are interested in the same goal of protecting the vulnerable.

The extent to which the absolutist and/or deontological nature of Aquinas' Natural Law works in contemporary society

REVISED

Contemporary society needs a deontological ethic	An absolutist ethic is useless in contemporary society	There is some value in rules for contemporary society
It is in the interest of justice that everyone follows the same rules in any society.	Society's needs have changed. Natural Law is unfair in modern life.	Natural Law seeks justice, so it can inform our decisions in normal circumstances.
Modern society is too egocentric and needs a moral authority.	Individual autonomy and personal well-being are better guides than rigid rules.	Moral laws balance our desire for personal freedom.
Modern society risks forgetting the purpose of morality – to do good, to avoid evil.	Moral problems are rarely binary now, e.g. abortion is a complex dilemma.	Some basic rules and laws prevent society from descending into anarchy.
The individual cannot be trusted to reason correctly. Rules are simpler.	A compassionate response to contemporary problems is needed (e.g. euthanasia).	Some actions are intrinsically wrong, while others may be up to individuals to choose.

The strengths and weaknesses of Aquinas' Natural Law

The strengths of Natural Law outweigh its weaknesses	The weaknesses of Natural Law outweigh its strengths	The strengths and weaknesses are equally balanced
Natural Law offers a clear ethical system that is easy to follow.	Natural Law is complex and difficult to work out. It would be easy to get it wrong.	Ethical problems are complex. Moral Laws must reflect this but also be practical.
It is holistic, supporting the needs of the agent through virtues, not just policing acts.	It does not look at the unique moral situation, so it does not support people's needs at all.	No theory can meet every unique need, but policing character is a bridge too far.
It is just because it applies the same rule to everyone, no matter who they are.	Justice gives people the tools they need for success, not the same rules no matter what.	No ethical theory can both apply laws and allow for each unique situation.
It is rooted in scripture, meaning that it is in accordance with God's will.	Not everyone is religious. Natural Law's focus on God is meaningless to many.	Not everyone wants to follow God. This would also be true if it were a secular theory.

A consideration of whether Aquinas' Natural Law promotes injustice

The ethical theory of Natural Law promotes injustice	Natural Law does not promote injustice	Natural Law allows injustice but does not promote it
It forces people to perform actions that are not beneficial for them.	A complex situation does not negate the need for a fair universal law.	Natural Law provides a reasonable solution within which there may be casualties.
The laws it produces discriminate against gender and sexual orientation.	Natural Law promotes equal treatment rather than bending to the whims of society.	Natural Law's secondary precepts encourage flexibility but are open to manipulation.
It forces duties upon people (e.g. the duty to live, not the right to choose life).	Natural Law gives all people the same rights and responsibilities. This is fair.	Some people have more burdens than others. Natural Law allows them to suffer.
Some people are valued more than others, e.g. the unborn child is valued more than the woman.	The virtue of justice is written right into the system.	Natural Law unintentionally marginalises some as a side effect of protecting others.

The effectiveness of Aquinas' Natural Law in dealing with ethical issues

Aquinas is very effective in dealing with ethical issues	Aquinas is ineffective in dealing with ethical issues	Aquinas is partially effective in dealing with ethical issues
The primary precepts establish flexible, adaptable secondary precepts to suit the dilemma.	Natural Law does not consider additional issues, such as quality of life in issues such as euthanasia.	Rules are usually helpful, but virtuous, loving people put laws aside sometimes.
Natural Law is practical because it treats everyone the same.	It is patriarchal, putting women at a disadvantage in reproductive issues.	Treating everyone the same is usually ethical, but Natural Law suits men's needs better.
Natural Law protects the vulnerable, e.g. terminally ill or unborn people.	It has no flexibility to protect in extreme cases, e.g. rape or unmanageable pain.	More than one side can need protection. Woman and foetus are vulnerable in pregnancy.
Double effect resolves a conflict of precepts, making it more effective.	Double effect is just a loophole; it makes Natural Law hypocritical.	If we can make exceptions for double effect, why not elsewhere?

The extent to which Aquinas' Natural Law is meaningless without a belief in a creator God

REVISED

Natural Law requires a belief in God as creator	Natural Law works without a belief in God	A belief in God makes sense but is not required
The foundation of Natural Law is in Eternal and Divine Law, which require God.	Reason is the basis of the precepts. This is different from divine commands.	While God is the basis, it is possible to follow the laws without faith.
Worship God is an absolute precept. Natural Law collapses if we dispense with it.	Belief in God is a small part of Natural Law; there is much more to it than this.	Precepts are rights not duties. We have a right to worship God, but no requirement.
Absolute laws have authority only if there is a guarantor in the form of God.	Acts can have intrinsic worth even if there is no God to judge us.	The atheist is just as capable of valuing life and an ordered society as the religious person.
Natural Law is theocentric. Fellowship with God is the purpose of the entire theory.	Natural Law is reason-centric, based on empiricist, Aristotelian logic.	Aquinas' Natural Law requires God, but Finnis' version (see page 50) has no need for God.

Specimen exam questions

Sample AO1 questions

1 Outline the laws and precepts found in Aquinas' Natural Law. **(AS only)**
2 Examine the role of rational thought in Aquinas' Natural Law.
3 Explain the role of the seven virtues in Aquinas' Natural Law.
4 Apply Aquinas' Natural Law to the issue of voluntary euthanasia.

Sample AO2 questions

1 Evaluate the view that Aquinas' Natural Law requires belief in a creator God to make sense.
2 'Aquinas' virtues are ineffective in addressing the issue of abortion.' Evaluate this view.

> **Revision tip**
>
> An outline question will only appear in AS, never in A-level exam questions. This is because A-level responses always require more depth, so 'explain' or 'examine' will require detail and exemplification.

> **Revision tip**
>
> You could be asked to evaluate any part of the material on Natural Law from strands A–C. It is a good idea to engage with the material as you go along so that you know what you think of it, and why, when you get into the exam.

2D John Finnis' development of Natural Law

Who is John Finnis?

John Finnis (1940–present day) is an Australian legal philosopher and jurist. He is professor emeritus in the faculty of law at Oxford University and is the author of *Natural Law and Natural Rights* (1980, 2011). His work has been a major contribution to the Philosophy of Law and is a redevelopment of Aquinas' Natural Law.

Development of the seven basic human goods

REVISED

Finnis, like Aristotle, begins by asking what makes a worthwhile life. According to Finnis, there are seven basic goods or values for humankind. Features of the goods are that they are:

- intrinsically good
- all equally good
- universal to all cultures
- self-evident
- not based on anything else
- objectively and fundamentally true.

Actions are right or worthwhile only if they serve one or more of these seven goods:

1 **Life** – including self-preservation, freedom from pain, bodily health, freedom to procreate, marriage between a man and woman.
2 **Knowledge** – to comprehend and make sense of the world and our existence in it.
3 **Play** – seeking fun for its own sake.
4 **Aesthetic experience** – an appreciation of beauty, both in the natural world and in that which we create ourselves.
5 **Friendship** – peace and harmony between people, altruism.
6 **Practical reasonableness** – the working out of how to put a basic good into practice.
7 **Religion** – the freedom to have a harmony between the self and a non-human reality that gives meaning and purpose to life.

The basic goods are basic reasons for action. They explain why we should act. Laws give a structure to pursuing these seven goods. We have a duty to obey any law that coincides with pursuing these seven goods for ourselves, or for the rest of the community.

Distinction between theoretical/ practical reason

REVISED

Theoretical reason and practical reason have different applications and purposes.

Theoretical reason	Practical reason
Describes what is true.	Describes how to act.
Relies on some self-evident principles to be able to pursue knowledge, e.g. what constitutes a valid argument.	Takes the self-evident basic goods and establishes how to put them into practice in reality.
Cannot produce contradictory statements – one of the statements will be wrong.	Can produce contradictory acts. This offers us a choice of which we would like to follow.
Assesses the way things are.	Assesses what to do.
Reasoning leads to understanding.	Reasoning leads to actions.

Now test yourself

TESTED ☐

1 List the seven basic goods.
2 How do we know what the seven basic goods are?
3 Who do the goods apply to?

Nine requirements of practical reason

REVISED ☐

One of the basic goods is practical reason. This is a kind of legal reasoning. Practical reason is universal and timeless. To participate in the good of practical reason, you need to make rational decisions that will lead you to participate in the other six goods. It is the working out of the reasons why we should act followed by establishing the options for action that are guided by those reasons. Although Finnis realises that emotions play a part in decision-making, correct practical reasoning should not be ruled or distracted by them.

> **Revision tip**
>
> If you find it difficult to remember all nine requirements of practical reason, try to reduce each one to a single memorable word or an icon that will jog your memory.

The nine requirements are as follows:

1	Have a coherent plan of life	View life as a whole, plan commitments properly and don't live purely in the moment.
2	No arbitrary preferences among values	Prioritising of goods is necessary but must be rational and never reject a good outright.
3	No arbitrary preferences among persons	Goods should be available to everyone equally, be impartial (the Golden Rule).
4	Detachment	Don't fixate on a project, avoid fanaticism so that life isn't meaningless when a project ends.
5	Commitment	Don't abandon commitments lightly, be faithful to a project.
6	Efficiency within reason	Actions should be effective/fit for purpose/efficient in achieving basic goods.
7	Respect for every basic value in every act	Don't actively damage a basic good. All goods should be respected in every act.
8	The requirements of the common good	Foster the goods for everyone in the community.
9	Follow one's conscience	Even though conscience can make errors, never do something you believe is wrong.

You do have freedom in your choice-making. Some actions may go against a basic good, in which case they are wrong. However, you can freely choose from a range of activities that support the basic goods.

The common good

One of the requirements of practical reason is that the basic goods are for everyone. This is called the common good. Humans need to live together and co-operate with each other, for our own well-being and the well-being of everyone around us. If society is unfulfilled, then I am less likely to be fulfilled.

It serves the common good if everyone can seek the seven basic goods **autonomously**. The law can help us to achieve this and make sure that everyone has a fair chance of pursuing these goods. It would not serve the common good to treat some people preferentially because we like them. While it can be acceptable to treat people differently, if it fulfils the common good, it is essential that everyone in the community has an equal chance of pursuing the seven basic goods for themselves.

> **Autonomously** – the freedom to act independently and make one's own choices.

Now test yourself

TESTED

1 List the nine requirements of practical reason.
2 Give three ways in which practical reason differs from theoretical reason.
3 What is the relationship between emotion and reason in moral decision-making?
4 Why is practical reason useful?

The need for authority

Finnis claims that there is a difference between morality and law, but that where the two overlap is what gives law its full force. A moral theory like Natural Law establishes what is good, and law provides rules that allow us to co-ordinate with each other and resolve disputes. Where a law helps people collaborate to achieve the common good of everyone in line with the seven basic goods, then it is a good law.

An unjust law will prevent the basic goods being achieved, but it is still a law. We might still be obliged to obey an unjust law if by breaking it we would threaten the common good. For example, disobedience might break down the system of authority and make it harder to co-ordinate everyone.

The advantage of authority is that you don't need **unanimity**. You just need a leader who acts as a co-ordinator to ensure everyone can be free to pursue the basic goods without preventing others from doing the same. A useful authority will co-ordinate the actions of a community while leaving individuals the freedom to pursue the basic goods autonomously.

> **Unanimity** – complete agreement or consensus.

Now test yourself

1 Why is the common good so important?
2 What is the difference between morality and law?
3 Should we obey an unjust law?
4 Give three features of a successful authority.

Revision activity

Design a revision poster that demonstrates the relationship between all the aspects of Finnis' Natural Law. Make sure it includes a clear list of the seven goods and nine requirements. It can be a flow diagram or a picture, whichever will help you to remember more effectively.

Apply your knowledge

1 Which of these actions would be morally acceptable according to Finnis' Natural Law?
   a Lying to your teacher to avoid reprimand
   b Playing a practical joke on a classmate
   c A parent preventing their teenager from attending a festival before exams
   d Protesting outside an abortion clinic
   e Having a pyjama day and watching Netflix
   f Skipping class to meet your girlfriend

Exam checklist

Can you:
● clearly explain who John Finnis is, but avoid too much detail about his life and works
● define the seven basic goods
● explain how Finnis arrives at them
● understand the difference between practical and theoretical reasoning
● explain the nine requirements of practical reason
● understand how the common good relates to the nine requirements and the seven goods
● explain the need for authority in this system
● give an example of behaviour that might be acceptable or unacceptable and state why?

Typical mistake

Students often find it difficult to see how all the distinct aspects of a theory relate to each other and so their answers can sometimes be disjointed or appear like a list of terms. Make sure you know how the common good relates to authority, the basic goods and practical reason.

2E Bernard Hoose's overview of the Proportionalist debate

Proportionalism originated from Roman Catholic scholarship in Europe and the USA. To state a complex debate simplistically, there are moral rules that apply universally, but if there is a proportionate reason, it could be right to break them.

> **Who is Bernard Hoose?**
> Hoose (1945–present day) is an English Roman Catholic scholar whose works include *Proportionalism: The American Debate and Its European Roots* (1987). This work is mostly a comment on the phenomenon of Proportionalism rather than a clear expounding of his own views.

As a hybrid of Natural Law, a deontological/ teleological ethic

`REVISED`

Hoose is clear that Proportionalism is viewed by itself and its opponents as a teleological theory. However, Proportionalists acknowledge that moral laws are absolute unless there is a proportionate reason to go against them. The proportionate reason depends upon the situation but must be significant to justify deviation from the law.

Hoose says that when weighing up the morality of an act, Proportionalists consider aspects such as:
- the act performed by the agent
- consequences
- intentions of the moral agent.

None of these should be neglected and it is insufficient to consider only one. Consequences and intentions are linked since an intention to act predicts consequences. Equally, the act performed and the intention are linked through the person or agent performing the act.

Deontological	Teleological
The agent has a duty to obey universal laws.	The agent's intention should be evaluated.
Natural moral laws are absolute.	The consequences of the action are part of what makes it right.
Greek: deon (duty)	Greek: telos (purpose/goal)

This approach is visible in the Thomist law of double effect or prioritising of secondary precepts. Proportionalists find Aquinas to be inconsistent in allowing theft to save a life yet condemning lying for the same purpose. Proportionalism attempts to resolve that inconsistency. Yet Proportionalism is rejected by the Roman Catholic Church for its emphasis on consequences.

A Proportionalist maxim

`REVISED`

The maxim for Proportionalists is that it is never right to go against a principle unless there is a proportionate reason which would justify it. For the most part, the deontological rules of Natural Law should be obeyed because they tell us the good thing to do. Only in the most unusual of circumstances is it acceptable to perform a bad action for a right reason.

In such circumstances, we must weigh up whether there is a proportionate reason for breaking the rule. This is through balancing the **value** against the **disvalue** gained in the act.

> **Value** – the increase in positive results and decrease in negative results from the action.
>
> **Disvalue** – the increase in negative results and decrease in positive results from the action.

This is not about making careful calculations according to a prescriptive formula. Our weighing up is through an instinctive knowledge that the action we will take will produce more value than following the existing rule.

However, Proportionalist R. Ginters gives five rules of preference for actions:

- an action that brings about more good than evil
- an action that maximises both quality and quantity of good where possible
- a value that is most fundamental or basic – such as life above all else
- the most practically achievable action
- an act that protects the most urgent need.

Distinction between an evil moral act and pre-moral/ontic evil

As we live in a fallen world, there are events or actions that contain pain or damage that make moral perfection impossible. Proportionalists call these events or actions **ontic** or **pre-moral** evils.

> On page 79 of *Proportionalism: The American Debate and Its European Roots*, Hoose gives the following example: Imagine a strong man, trained in martial arts, sees a weaker man strangling a child. The weaker man does not respond to appeals to stop and so force is needed.

In this example, the ontic or pre-moral evil is the use of violence against another person.

- Attacking the weaker man will inevitably cause pain and it is part of life in a fallen world that the only way to rescue the child is with physical force.
- It is an ontic good to save the child's life. We intuitively know this; it is a conditioned response that requires no reasoning.
- The act becomes morally evil if, when he uses violence, the strong man does it to impress the child's sister with his physical ability.
- If he intends to harm or get gratification from harming, this is a morally evil action.
- If removing the attacker from the child by force was done out of love for God's law to preserve life, then we can say it is a morally good action.

Evil moral act	Pre-moral/ontic evil
Intentional harm or damage	The lack of perfection in the created order
E.g. punching someone to cause them pain	E.g. natural evils – disease, earthquakes, etc.
Caused by people	The reality of sin in our social structures
An ontic evil + an evil intent	E.g. pain resulting from surgery
Immoral or sinful action	Harm or damage that is inevitable
Contains greater disvalue than value	Tolerable if for a proportionate reason

1 Define the terms deontological and teleological.
2 Explain when it would be acceptable to break a rule.

TESTED

Ontic/pre-moral evil – harmful events or actions that result from living in an imperfect, fallen world.

2E Bernard Hoose's overview of the Proportionalist debate

WJEC and Eduqas A level Religious Studies Religion and Ethics 55

Another example from Hoose (*Proportionalism*, pp. 44–45) is a surgeon cutting a patient's flesh. This is an ontic evil because it causes harm. If she does it to cure an illness, the act becomes morally good. We must weigh up the proportionate value against the disvalue caused by this act. It would be significant disvalue to perform this act to deal with a spot but would have value if it fixed a broken leg.

Now test yourself

TESTED ☐

Give three features of an evil moral act and three features of an ontic evil.

Revision activity

Look at the following examples and decide whether there could be a proportionate reason to break the rules:

1 A woman with an ectopic pregnancy that is threatening both her life and the child's – the law forbids abortion.
2 A serial killer arrives at your door looking for a man you know is hiding in your attic – the law forbids lying.
3 A taxi driver has a client who has been shot, is bleeding and needs to get to hospital – the law forbids speeding.

Identify what you think are the ontic evils and the moral evils or goods involved in each scenario.

Distinction between a good act and a right act

REVISED ☐

Hoose devotes a chapter of his book to the distinction between:

- a good act (an act that follows a moral principle and is performed out of love for God and his law)
- a right act (an act that could go against a moral principle, but for a proportionate reason, having weighed up all the foreseeable consequences and the proportionate value against the disvalue, e.g. harming another human to save the life of a child).

What is good is not necessarily the same as what is right. Our strong man attacks the weaker man, even though he knows it to be an ontic evil. He could be right to do so if the value of the action is greater than the disvalue.

Value	Consequence is that the child lives.
	Motive is from love for God's law to preserve life.
	The act of saving life is an ontic good.
Disvalue	The act of violence towards another is an ontic evil.
	The consequence is that the attacker is harmed.

This is therefore a right act, provided the violence used to save the child is proportionate. It would be acceptable to push the attacker away, but not to break out an atomic bomb!

Proportionality based on agape

Agape is what makes an ontic good into a moral good. However, terrible acts can be done from a loving motive. Love should motivate a good action but love alone won't make the action right. Love is about having a sincere search for the right moral behaviour, and it is this search that is the essence of Proportionalism.

While Proportionalism sounds quite like Situation Ethics, in that Fletcher was prepared to consider the rules until there was a loving reason to abandon them, it differs in a few ways:

- Situation Ethics considers love to be the only thing necessary to make an act morally good, whereas Proportionalism allows that a loving act can be an ontic evil and can be wrong if it has more disvalue than value.
- Unlike Fletcher, Proportionalists accept that there is such a thing as an intrinsically good or bad action but that a bad action can sometimes be right.

Apply your knowledge

Hoose considers an executioner (*Proportionalism*, pp. 47–48) who carries out capital punishment on criminals according to the direction of the courts of law.

- What would be the morally good action in this situation?
- What could be the motive if the executioner refused to carry out his duty?
- Identify the value and the disvalue if the executioner refuses to do his job.
- What is the right action for this executioner?

Exam checklist

Can you:

- define the terms deontological and teleological
- state which features of Proportionalism are deontological and which are teleological
- explain what is meant by proportionate reason
- explain the difference between an immoral or evil act and a pre-moral evil
- show the importance of intentions to Proportionalists
- define the difference between a good and a right act
- explain how to work out the value against the disvalue of an action
- show the importance of agape in Proportionalism
- give a worked example to demonstrate these features?

2F Finnis' Natural Law and Proportionalism – application of the theory

Immigration

REVISED

Immigration involves moving to live permanently in a country where the person is not a native and does not possess citizenship.

There is a wide range of reasons or push factors to explain why people would immigrate to the UK. These include, but are not restricted to:

- to join family who live here
- to work or receive education
- to escape poverty, war, natural disasters or persecution
- to access health care or other resources
- to avoid criminal justice or claim asylum.

Positive effects of immigration	Negative effects of immigration
Immigration can solve shortages in some UK jobs.	Immigration contributes to low wages where there is greater choice of workers.
It can save life or reduce suffering.	There is increased pressure on public services.
It can reduce spending on education for those who were educated elsewhere.	Immigration contributes to housing shortages.
Many immigrants want to make a positive contribution.	Language or cultural integration is challenging.
Many are prepared to work to have better lives.	Net growth of the economy is unsustainable.
Taxation applies to new workers as well.	Taxation cannot cover the cost of supporting people.

The application of Finnis' Natural Law to immigration

REVISED

Finnis made controversial statements in a 2009 article, stating that he believes we should be cautious with immigration law. He wrote that the UK culture and population were decaying, replaced by reverse colonisation, by other people, cultures, religions and ambitions, regardless of their worth. He claimed that this would lead to hatred and bloodshed as people failed to integrate successfully.

> Aashi is an Indian woman in her 20s. Her mother has died, she has no father and her brother has moved to London to work. She has little formal education and no job in her village but would like to move to be near her brother, who has agreed to support her while she looks for work. She does not speak English but is keen to learn.

Aashi should be allowed to come to live in the UK

Finnis' principle	How it is applied
Seven basic goods are universal	Aashi has the same rights to pursue the goods as everyone else.
Life, knowledge, play and friendship	The goods can be achieved more effectively in the UK with family.
Try to improve yourself	By hoping to come to the UK, Aashi is trying to improve her life.
View your life as a whole, plan your actions	She can learn a new language, skills and get work or access education.
Harm no basic goods	None of these actions harms a basic good for anyone else.

Aashi should not be allowed to come to live in the UK

Finnis' principle	How it is applied
Role of authority	Laws on immigration are needed to co-ordinate the common good.
Life	If Aashi's life were in danger, we could grant her asylum, but it is not.
Play, aesthetic experience, friendship and knowledge	Aashi is still free to pursue these if she stays in India.
Consider the big picture and plan effectively to produce the maximum good	The common good beyond Aashi's situation is to place laws to avoid excessive immigration.
Common good	More people coming to the UK puts pressure on public services and increases public spending.

The application of Proportionalism to immigration

There is no clearly recommended method of calculating what is proportionally right. We know instinctively which action lessens the disvalue in the world. Pragmatically, there should be regulation and control of immigration to ensure that there are enough resources for everyone to share, but if a case does not meet the control criteria, we need to weigh the value against the disvalue.

	Aashi comes to the UK	Aashi remains in India
Value	<ul><li>Her life is improved.</li><li>There is a loving motive to welcome her here.</li><li>Life prospects will be improved.</li><li>She can contribute to society.</li><li>It will enhance cultural diversity.</li></ul>	<ul><li>She can contribute to her existing community.</li><li>Her life is not endangered.</li><li>She can develop skills in situ.</li></ul>
Disvalue	<ul><li>Public resources are required to get her settled.</li><li>Her village is deprived of a contributor.</li><li>It sets a precedent for other family members to come.</li></ul>	<ul><li>She has no career prospects.</li><li>She has no means of protection or support.</li><li>She has no prospects available to improve her life.</li><li>Her village must support her or let her suffer.</li></ul>

Apply your knowledge

How would the answers to this example change (if at all) if Aashi was in one of the following situations:
a at risk due to war
b a highly educated doctor
c had no family in the UK
d a criminal?

Capital punishment

The death penalty is a government-sanctioned punishment, whereby a criminal is put to death. The UK no longer uses capital punishment, but many other countries do. Capital punishment in the modern world can be carried out by:

- lethal injection
- electrocution
- hanging
- gassing
- shooting
- beheading.

Such punishments are usually meted out to people convicted of murder, treason or other crimes against humanity.

Positive effects of capital punishment	Negative effects of capital punishment
It reduces public spending on imprisonment.	It is barbaric or inhumane.
It eases overcrowding in prisons.	It risks death after wrongful conviction.
It allows vengeance to be served.	Convict appeals clog up court systems.
It allows closure for families of victims.	It is irrational – don't kill or we will kill you.
It acts as a deterrent for other would-be criminals.	Proportionately more racial minorities are convicted.

The application of Finnis' Natural Law to capital punishment

Finnis rejects capital punishment because you cannot directly violate a basic good. The basic good here is that of life. This principle is universal so there are no exceptions, not even for a murderer. This contrasts with Aquinas, who argues that killing can be moral if performed by a legitimate authority.

Kamau has been convicted of murdering a police officer when he was confronted robbing a convenience store. He shows no remorse and, since being in custody, has been continually violent and abusive towards staff. The police officer leaves behind a widow and three young children.

Revision activity

Look in the newspapers and find current stories pertaining to immigration and capital punishment. How would Finnis and Proportionalists respond to them? Make sure that you use at least three of the key principles of each of their theories in your response.

For capital punishment	Against capital punishment
We must consider the common good of the whole society.	You cannot violate the basic good of life.
The authority must protect the common good. Some argue it should prioritise the lives of the community.	It would be possible to encourage Kamau to try to improve himself through rehabilitation.
Showing compassion to the officer's family and allowing them closure promotes friendship.	Natural Law is not about emotional responses, so you cannot meet injury with more injury.
We must look at the big picture and plan ahead to prevent the loss of future lives.	Death would make it impossible to pursue any other basic goods.

The application of Proportionalism to capital punishment

Punishment is an ontic evil because it causes suffering to another human being. We should weigh up the value and disvalue of capital punishment to decide whether it is morally right. Any punishment which does not benefit the recipient is problematic for Hoose. Dangerous criminals who are unmoved by attempts to help them need imprisoning for public safety, but inhumane treatment is unjustified. This rules out capital punishment.

In Hoose's *Christian Ethics: An Introduction*, Chapter 14, he gives three justifications for capital punishment and why he rejects them. Applying these to the example of Kamau, we can use Proportionalism to argue for capital punishment too:

> **Apply your knowledge**
>
> What aspects of Finnis' Natural Law or Proportionalism have not been mentioned in the answer in the table below? What could you add to improve these responses?

Motives for punishment	Can capital punishment achieve this?
Deterrence/prevention	No: Using Kamau to scare others does not value life. The threat of capital punishment did not deter Kamau from crime. We can protect society and minimise ontic evil through imprisonment.
	Yes: If the punishment is painless, private and dignified, we avoid moral evil. This causes the minimum disvalue necessary to provide the value of protecting society.
Retribution/restitution	No: Kamau cannot replace the life he took. To tell whether any form of capital punishment would proportionally fit Kamau's crime, we must consider all that drove him to kill. It would be unloving to neglect this appraisal.
	Yes: It is proportionally appropriate (a life for a life). Less punishment would limit the amount of value gained from punishing him at all.
Reform/rehabilitation	No: Capital punishment cannot reform Kamau or benefit him in any way. Reform can bring about value only when it causes the minimum harm possible to achieve its aims.
	Yes: If we accept the belief in an afterlife with God, then Kamau's death sentence could encourage him to repent of his sins before God and reform as he prepares for death.

> **Typical mistake**
>
> Avoid focusing your essay on the opinions of Finnis/Hoose. Marks are awarded for your application of the theory, not just the conclusion.

Exam checklist

Can you:
- explain the fundamental issues that arise in arguments about immigration
- explain the key issues that arise in arguments about capital punishment
- describe the main principles of Finnis' and Hoose's moral theories
- show how these principles could mean that immigration is right or that it is wrong
- show how these principles could mean that capital punishment is right or that it is wrong?

Issues for analysis and evaluation

There are six issues for analysis and evaluation listed on the specification as examples of the kinds of AO2 questions you could be asked. Consider the possible conclusions to the question before you establish your lines of reasoning. Develop these lines of argument by giving examples or evidence to demonstrate the points.

Whether Finnis' Natural Law is acceptable in contemporary society

REVISED

Finnis' Natural Law is acceptable in contemporary society	Finnis' Natural Law is unacceptable in contemporary society	Finnis' Natural Law has some useful elements
It allows people the freedom to choose from a wide range of appropriate goods.	Absolutism is discriminatory. E.g. Men have more choices than women who must neglect their own good for the good of the unborn.	It demonstrates that there can be more than one way to perform a good action.
The goods include things like play and friendship, which we value highly today.	There is no reason to accept the goods as absolute. There is no basis for them.	We can prioritise goods provided it is rational and we do not damage other goods.
A co-ordinating authority encourages positive co-operation, not resistance.	It is unrealistic for authority to never sacrifice an individual for the common good.	It still gives some guidance that is needed for co-operation in a large community.
Finnis shares the value of practical reason with contemporary society.	The vagueness of the goods gives the illusion of freedom, without the reality.	Natural Law preserves the same things as the Universal Declaration of Human Rights.

The extent to which Proportionalism promotes immoral behaviour

REVISED

Proportionalism promotes immoral behaviour	Proportionalism does not promote immoral behaviour	Proportionalism inadvertently allows immorality
The good/right distinction is an exercise in semantics to excuse evil acts.	The good/right distinction encourages people to perform the lesser of two ontic evils.	Proportionalists do not promote bad actions but allow them when they are necessary.
Proportionalists reject moral absolutes by giving too much weight to consequences.	Proportionalists do not weigh up consequences alone, but also acts, values and intentions.	Proportionalists intend compassion in weighing up of consequences, but they are unpredictable.
Proportionalism prioritises reason above the absolute laws set by God.	We should lovingly obey God's laws, unless the circumstances are extreme.	Reason can be wrong. By following it, we could perform innately wrong acts.
It gives permission to perform any act at all if we can give enough reasons for it.	Most, not all, actions can be justified for their loving consequences.	We might all judge value and disvalue in different ways.

Whether Finnis and/or Proportionalism provide a basis for moral decision-making for believers and/or non-believers

REVISED

Finnis provides a strong basis for believers/non-believers	Proportionalism provides a strong basis for believers/non-believers	Neither theory provides a strong basis for morality
There is no direct mention of God in Finnis' Natural Law, so non-believers could use it.	There is nothing to stop atheists from weighing up value against disvalue.	They both eventually include reference to God or religion, so are inaccessible to atheists.
It is compatible with a belief in God since it is a development of Thomist Natural Law.	This is also a development of Thomist Law, Aquinas required proportionate responses.	These theories are more aspirational than a clear set of structured laws.
The idea of strict laws is appealing to anyone who wants clear guidance.	Proportionalism could be used in relation to any system of law, with or without God.	Natural Law depends upon an unproven assumption that we all have a common purpose.
Authority is bestowed on Human Law but can ultimately be derived from God.	Authority is given to the individual to weigh up value against disvalue.	Proportionalism is rejected by the Roman Catholic Church as allowing any action.

The strengths and weaknesses of Finnis' Natural Law and/or Proportionalism

REVISED

The strengths/weaknesses of Finnis' Natural Law	The strengths/weaknesses of Proportionalism
It is based on values that contemporary society find important.	It is based on common sense rather than blind obedience to impersonal laws.
It allows us freedom to choose between acts that are good, rather than forcing action.	It allows the use of reason rather than blind obedience.
It still controls our behaviour through restrictive, unbending laws.	The laws have little authority even though we are required to obey them in the first instance.
The goods are appealing but not moral laws. How is the requirement to play a moral one?	Predicting consequences involves guesswork, so Proportionalism has a weak basis.

The effectiveness of Finnis' Natural Law and/or Proportionalism in dealing with ethical issues

REVISED

The effectiveness of Finnis' Natural Law	The effectiveness of Proportionalism	One is more effective than the other
Finnis deals with capital punishment by ensuring basic goods are available to all.	The differentiation between good and right is effective in extreme situations.	Proportionalism is impractical by rejecting punishment altogether.
Finnis allows freedom to consider immigration in each community.	Proportionalists allow communities to weigh up value against disvalue in immigration cases.	Proportionalism is less dehumanising and considers reasons for immigration.
Finnis' system is thorough but does not lend itself to decision-making in an emergency.	Proportionalism relies on intuition more than a strict system so could enable quick decisions.	Finnis is unable to view non-western culture as offering opportunities for good.
There is diversity not consistency when individuals try to apply practical reason.	Proportionalism relies on individuals using common sense. We don't all have this.	Finnis is practical in being able to co-ordinate communities with authority.

The extent to which Finnis' Natural Law is a better ethic than Proportionalism or vice versa

Finnis' Natural Law is better than Hoose's Proportionalism	Proportionalism ethic is better than Finnis' Natural Law	They are both equally strong/ weak
Finnis is better in giving a reason for authority without resorting to God.	Proportionalism values the authority of God's law, but gives flexibility when options are limited.	Both theories give a strong basis for moral action using reason, God or both.
Finnis is better in applying consistent criteria to all decisions. This is fair.	Proportionalism gives a system but also has space for other human attributes, like intuition.	Both theories are systematic and for the most part agree on what is good.
Finnis allows all people to have access to basic goods without discrimination.	Proportionalism even values the goods for the criminal so is unconditional in his values.	Both theories are idealistic as all people cannot have access to all the goods all the time.
Finnis is better because his goods allow for a high quality of life not just quantity.	Proportionalism acknowledges moral complexity by weighing value against disvalue.	Both theories ultimately place human reason above God's divine commands.

Specimen exam questions

Sample AO1 questions

1 Compare Finnis' Natural Law with the Proportionalist approach to ethics.
2 Examine the place of the nine requirements of practical reason in Finnis' Natural Law.
3 Explain the deontological and teleological features of Proportionalism.
4 Apply Finnis' Natural Law to the ethical issue of immigration.

Sample AO2 questions

1 Evaluate how acceptable Finnis' Natural Law is for contemporary society.
2 'Proportionalism is ineffective in dealing with capital punishment.' Evaluate this view.

Revision tip

Ensure you can use the technical vocabulary from Finnis' Natural Law and Proportionalism when applying them to the issues of immigration and capital punishment. It is important not to give generalised responses.

Revision tip

It is reasonable to make use of scholars from other areas of the specification to help you answer an AO2 question if using them enables you to challenge or support the question.

Theme 3 Teleological ethics

There are several different normative ethical theories that can be described as teleological. You will need to be able to talk about Situation Ethics and Utilitarianism as teleological theories. A teleological ethic focuses on the goal of an action rather than the action itself. For the Situation Ethicist, any moral action must have love as its goal or purpose. Other teleological theories will have different goals. In Utilitarianism, the goal is happiness.

3A Joseph Fletcher's Situation Ethics – his rejection of other forms of ethics and his acceptance of agape as the basis of morality

Who was Joseph Fletcher?
Joseph Fletcher (1905–1991) was an American Episcopalian priest and professor. He lectured in Christian ethics and medical ethics and wrote *Situation Ethics: The New Morality* in 1966. He founded the ethical theory Situation Ethics.

Fletcher was writing post-war, when society was rejecting the rigidity of **legalist** systems, like Natural Law. Society wanted to break free from the restrictive lifestyle that rationing and war life tended to bring with it. He was also responding to the more **antinomian**, free love movement and **existentialist** philosophy that encouraged people to create themselves, without guidance from authority.

> **Agape** – selfless/ unconditional care or concern for others.
>
> **Legalism** – a strict set of prefabricated laws or rules that are absolute in nature and cannot be broken.
>
> **Antinomianism** – literally, lawless; the lack of any rules or guidance at all.
>
> **Existentialism** – rejects pre-existent soul/purpose; instead, we create our own 'self'.

Fletcher's rejection of other approaches within ethics: legalism, antinomianism

REVISED

Fletcher rejected legalism because:
- it was too restrictive
- it lacked compassion for the challenges people faced
- it put laws before people
- it led to immorality by forcing people to obey laws even when it harmed them.

Fletcher rejected antinomianism because:
- it was 'ad hoc' or random in its approach
- it would lead to chaos/anarchy
- it did not protect the vulnerable members of society
- it was inconsistent and unprincipled.

> **Now test yourself**
> 1 What is meant by the term antinomian?
> 2 Why did Fletcher reject legalism?
>
> TESTED

The role of conscience

Fletcher felt that conscience was valuable in moral decision-making, but rejected the definitions given by other thinkers. Our conscience does not direct us; instead, it is a process that we go through when we apply our reasoning to a specific problem that needs to be solved.

What conscience is not:	What conscience is:
God's voice/supernatural guide	A verb not a noun (it isn't a thing we are naming, it is an action we are doing)
Backward-looking, assessing things you have done/guilt	Creative, flexible and forward-looking
Intuition or radar that instinctively knows what is right or wrong	Practical, problem-solving

Typical mistake

Don't make the mistake of writing that Fletcher rejected rules entirely. He only advocated going against societal norms when it best served love.

Fletcher's rationale for using the religious concept of 'agape' as the middle way between the extremes of legalism and antinomianism

Agape allows people the flexibility to approach moral situations without having to stick rigidly to potentially outdated laws. It gives guidance and protection to people and is consistent with Jesus' behaviour, so it is attractive to Christians. When making decisions about how to behave, people should:
- stick to society's laws unless it seems more loving to break them
- have love as the main goal of every moral action.

It is important to understand what agape is not. The ancient Greeks had several words that can all be translated into English as love.
1 Storge – instinctive love, like a parent for a child. A feeling that just comes to you.
2 Philios – love for friends, a love you choose that might be dependent upon their behaviour towards you.
3 Eros – romantic or sexual love, as you might have for a lover. It is sometimes confused with lust.
4 Agape – none of the above. It is an action of care or concern for another being that is not dependent upon whether they are a nice person or not. It is more like our understanding of the word charity.

Fletcher felt that agape was the best way to make moral decisions because:
- it does not discriminate against people
- it shows compassion to all people equally
- it is a firm principle upon which to base all behaviour, so avoids the chaos of antinomianism
- it is flexible, showing love to people in different ways, depending on who they are and what their situation is. This avoids the rigidity of legalism.

The biblical evidence used to support this approach

New Testament evidence for agape is plentiful. Good examples of Jesus showing agape could be as follows:

Synopsis	Bible reference
Jesus rescues a woman caught in adultery from being stoned. He forgives her.	John 8:1–11
Jesus heals a man with a withered hand on the Sabbath when it is forbidden to work.	Mark 3:1–6
Jesus teaches we should love our enemies.	Luke 6:27–36

The exam specification tells us that there are two passages that should be considered.

The teachings of Jesus (Luke 10:25–37)

Jesus teaches that agape is scripturally based. He tells a story to show that true obedience to this law of love may be unconventional in its application.

The Parable of the Good Samaritan (synopsis)
- A lawyer tests Jesus by asking how to inherit eternal life.
- Jesus asks what is written in the law.
- The lawyer replies with the Shema: 'You shall love the Lord your God with all your heart, soul, strength and mind; and your neighbour as yourself.'
- Jesus confirms this.
- The lawyer asks, 'Who is my neighbour?'
- Jesus replies with a parable: A Levite man travelling from Jerusalem to Jericho was attacked by robbers, who left him for dead. A priest and later a Levite saw him and passed by without helping. But a travelling Samaritan saw him and helped (Samaritans and Levites were enemies). He treated the victim's wounds, found him an inn, cared for him, then paid the innkeeper to shelter the victim until he was well.
- Jesus asks who was the most neighbourly.
- The lawyer identifies the Samaritan.
- Jesus tells him to do likewise.

The teachings of St Paul (1 Corinthians 13)

This passage on love is often read at weddings, but it is talking about more than romantic love. Paul lists the qualities required by agape that are not about feelings so much as they are about charitable behaviour towards other people.

St Paul's teaching on love (synopsis)

Paul lists the following actions:

1 Speaking in tongues
2 Prophetic powers
3 Knowledge
4 Faith
5 Giving away possessions
6 Giving up your life

These are all worthless without love. All these things come to an end. All these things are limited.

Love is:	Love is not:	Love does not:	Love does:
patient	envious	rejoice in wrongdoing	rejoice in the truth
kind	boastful	insist on its own way	bear all things
greater than faith	arrogant		believe all things
greater than hope	rude		hope all things
	irritable		endure all things
	resentful		never end

Revision activity

Draw a simple diagram to show the relationship between legalism, antinomianism and agape. Include a list of the key features of each approach.

Situation Ethics as a form of moral relativism   REVISED

Moral relativism is the stance that there are no absolute moral rules or laws, but that all decisions should be made in relation to the extent to which (in this case) love is achieved. This means that we can abandon a law that says, 'You shall not lie with a male as with a woman; it is an abomination' (Leviticus 18:22, NRSV) if, and only if, it is more loving to do so. In contrast, an absolutist stance says that we must obey that law regardless of circumstances.

A consequentialist theory   REVISED

Consequentialism assesses moral actions based on their *outcome* or *results* rather than the act itself. Situation Ethics, as a consequentialist theory, works out whether the result of an act will be loving. If it is, then it is a good act. An act, such as sex between members of the same gender, is neither intrinsically good nor intrinsically bad. It is dependent upon the outcome of the act in each separate case.

A teleological theory   REVISED

Teleological theories focus upon an act's *purpose* or *goal*. Situation Ethics is teleological because it aims for love in its decision-making process.

Apply your knowledge

Some people would argue that some actions are intrinsically wrong, and Situation Ethics encourages immoral behaviour. Think of a worked example where a loving action might be morally terrible.

Typical mistake

Many students will state that Situation Ethics is consequentialist and teleological, and then will define the two words together as though they mean exactly the same thing. There is a difference – consequentialist means focused on results, teleological is goal-focused. Define these words separately.

Exam checklist

Can you:

- define the following terms: legalism, antinomianism, agape, conscience, relativism, consequentialist, teleological
- describe the content of Luke 10:25–37 and 1 Corinthians 13
- list three reasons why Fletcher did not like legalism
- list three reasons why Fletcher did not like antinomianism
- explain what agape is *not*
- explain what a conscience does?

3B Fletcher's Situation Ethics – the principles as a means of assessing morality

The boss principle of Situation Ethics (following the concept of agape)

REVISED ☐

- Agape is the unconditional care or concern for others/altruistic behaviour/charity.
- The boss principle is the leading or fundamental principle.
- Agape is the overriding principle that has priority over all other laws.
- Any law that does not serve love can be broken.
- This principle is sometimes called the agapeistic calculus – greatest love for the greatest number.
- Sometimes Situation Ethics is called Christian Utilitarianism.

The four working principles

REVISED ☐

These principles were provided by Fletcher to guide people in how they can best be loving. They are not rules or laws; they describe how love should be applied.

1 **P**ragmatism – (practicality) any action must be practically possible in working to serve a loving outcome.
2 **P**ersonalism – (people before law) the individual person is the priority and love for them is more important than the detail of any law.
3 **P**ositivism – (faith first) you cannot prove that love is the most important thing. We must just have faith that it is and then apply our reason afterwards to see how best to be loving.
4 **R**elativism – (no set rules) all acts must be relative to a loving outcome. There are no fixed laws that apply universally except for love.

The six fundamental principles

REVISED ☐

These six principles are not laws or rules; they give guidance regarding how best to be loving when faced with a moral dilemma.

1 **O**nly love – the only intrinsically good thing is love and nothing else.
2 **R**uling norm – love is the ruling norm of Christian decision-making. For a Christian to make a moral decision, they must always assess whether it will produce love before they worry about whether it obeys laws like the ten commandments.
3 **J**ustice = love – love and justice are the same thing. Justice is love shared out fairly.
4 **N**eighbourly love – love your neighbour as you love yourself.
5 **E**nds justify the means – if the outcome is loving, any action at all is permitted.
6 **S**ituation – acts should be decided situationally not prescriptively. This means we look to the situation and decide each individual case, rather than looking to a prefabricated set of rules and trying to make them fit the circumstances.

Now test yourself

1 What is a boss principle?
2 What does positivism mean?
3 Which of the six fundamental principles were evident in Luke 10:25–37 and 1 Corinthians 13

TESTED ☐

Typical mistake

Watch your definition of positivism. Many students get this wrong and make up the idea that people must have a positive attitude. Look carefully at the definition and learn it by heart.

Apply your knowledge

Fletcher gives the example of a schizophrenic woman who is raped while in care and becomes pregnant. Natural Law would forbid abortion. Using the principles, explain why it might be loving to allow it.

Exam checklist

Can you:
- define the following terms: boss principle, agape, pragmatism, positivism, relativism, personalism
- describe the six fundamental principles
- use and apply the following terms: altruistic, prescriptive, intrinsic
- show the principles that are evident in the Bible passages from the previous section?

3C Fletcher's Situation Ethics – application of the theory

The application of Fletcher's Situation Ethics to homosexual relationships

Homosexuality includes some, but not necessarily all, of the following things:
- a sexual relationship between humans of the same gender
- a romantic relationship between humans of the same gender
- a commitment, such as marriage or civil partnership, between humans of the same gender.

What does religion teach?

The **Abrahamic** faiths include the following teachings relating to homosexuality:

> 'Therefore, a man leaves his father and his mother and clings to his wife, and they become one flesh.'
>
> Genesis 2:24 (NRSV)
>
> 'God blessed them, and God said to them, "Be fruitful and multiply, and fill the earth and subdue it."'
>
> Genesis 1:28 (NRSV)
>
> 'You shall not lie with a male as with a woman; it is an abomination.'
>
> Leviticus 18:22 (NRSV)

Abrahamic – religions based on the life of Abraham (Judaism, Islam and Christianity).

Other world faiths do not necessarily clearly condemn or uphold homosexuality. But at some stage, all have made statements that say homosexuality is against the tenets of their faith.

What would Fletcher say?

Any laws or rules against homosexuality take second place to the command to love. **(The first and second fundamental principles dictate this.)** So, if it is more loving to allow homosexual acts than to prohibit them, then they should be allowed.

Revision tip

Include worked examples. These can be taken from real life or from fiction. The important thing is that you can show how to use Situation Ethics to make a moral decision.

Is homosexual sex ethically acceptable?

> Kai is gay. He is planning a night out and hopes to meet someone at some point in the evening who might be interested in casual sex. He does not wish to have a relationship at present.
>
> Aylin is gay. She is in a long-term relationship and has been with her girlfriend for five years. She would like to propose and eventually start a family together. They have an active sex life.

Kai	Aylin
Pragmatism – this is not a practical way to achieve agape; it is more akin to lust. Although it could be loving to allow someone to express themselves sexually.	**Pragmatism** – practically, this is a useful way to ensure that agape is achieved. Care or concern for your spouse and their needs is part of what is required within a marriage.
Personalism – it is up to Kai to decide what makes him feel fulfilled. In his unique situation, he does not feel fulfilment through sex with women.	**Personalism** – we cannot dictate that they get married. We should look at their unique situation and respond to their needs and wishes.
Love = justice – we should apply the same principles here as we do to heterosexual sex. If Kai and his partner both consent to casual sex, it may not be unloving to accept it.	**Love = justice** – we should apply the principles as we would to a heterosexual couple. Marriage and starting a family will result in agape regardless of sexuality.
The ends justify the means – if the result is courteous treatment and respect for both, then it is acceptable. If Kai intends to use his partner to get his own way, this is not agapeic.	**The ends justify the means** – having children involves the couple sharing their love for each other with a child. More love is achieved than by sticking rigidly to religious laws.
Love your neighbour as yourself – Kai should plan to treat his partner as he wants to be treated. If it is likely that he will cause harm to his partner, then he should avoid sex.	**Love your neighbour as yourself** – if Aylin is prepared to prioritise her girlfriend's well-being and the well-being of their future children, then this is a morally good and loving act.

Now test yourself

TESTED ☐

1 Which of the principles of Situation Ethics are not mentioned in the examples above?
2 How could you apply them to this example?

Apply your knowledge

Can you use Situation Ethics to forbid the marriage of Aylin and her girlfriend? Why/why not?

The application of Fletcher's Situation Ethics to polyamorous relationships

REVISED ☐

- A polyamorous relationship is the idea that more than two people are willingly and knowledgably involved in a sexual and/or romantic relationship with each other.
- It has been around since ancient Greek times but is gaining more attention in the modern world.
- It requires honesty and consent from everyone within the relationship.
- It is not usually purely sexual in nature, so rejects casual sex, cheating or swinging.
- It has no clear boundaries or definitions that have been universally agreed upon.

What does religion teach?

Christian tradition prohibits these kinds of relationships, but there is no clarity in scripture since it is not mentioned specifically. The New Testament refers to Bishops and Deacons only marrying once. In the Old Testament, key figures were married more than once. This is not necessarily reference to polyamory though.

> 'Therefore, a man leaves his father and his mother and clings to his wife, and they become one flesh.'
>
> Genesis 2:24 (NRSV)
>
> 'For this is the will of God, your sanctification: that you abstain from fornication.'
>
> 1 Thessalonians 4:3 (NRSV)
>
> 'Let marriage be held in honour by all and let the marriage bed be kept undefiled; for God will judge fornicators and adulterers.'
>
> Hebrews 13:4 (NRSV)

However, God appears to allow polygamy in the Old Testament at key times to protect vulnerable women, e.g. to provide for those who have been widowed.

> 'If he takes another wife to himself, he shall not diminish the food, clothing, or marital rights of the first wife.'
>
> Exodus 21:10 (NRSV)

Other faiths may have traditions of polygamy, but these are not necessarily the same thing as polyamorous relationships. Polygamy includes a marital commitment. However, polyamory does not require this and is **gender fluid**.

Gender fluid – not restricted by social conception of gender (in this case, meaning that there is no fixed definition of how many people of which genders may be involved).

What would Fletcher say?

Any laws or rules about polyamorous relationships are of secondary importance to love. We must start from a position where we trust that love is the good thing (positivism) and then work out how best to be loving. We need to assess the individual situation (relativism).

Is a polyamorous relationship ethically acceptable?

> Iker, Mina and Jax met and shared digs at university. Their friendship gradually became deeply emotional and sexual. Now each feels distressed at the thought of being apart. They wish to continue living together as sexual and romantic partners after university.

Yes	No
Pragmatism – this relationship does not affect anyone else. It would ensure emotional and physical fulfilment for all three members of their group.	**Pragmatism** – it would be very challenging to legislate for such a relationship. There is no way to protect people from being pressured into this kind of relationship.
Personalism/love decides situationally – in their situation, they are all consenting and desirous of the relationship; their needs must be put before law.	**Personalism/love decides situationally** – in their situation they say there will be more love, but it is not the kind of love that Fletcher was talking about. This is eros not agape.

Yes	No
Love = justice – we should treat them fairly. We don't require a monogamous, heterosexual couple to give up their lives together, so it may be unfair to ask it of these people.	**Love = justice** – we are not denying anyone a loving relationship. Fairness requires that each person gives their attention to one person at a time, regardless of sexual orientation.
The ends justify the means – the outcome would be for happiness and emotional/sexual fulfilment. Resulting children will have three loving parents to care for them.	**The ends justify the means** – the outcome is unpredictable. Any resulting children could lead to the exclusion of whichever person is not biologically related. This is not agapeic.
Love your neighbour as yourself – if each of them feels that they can put the needs of the other two before their own, then agape can be served through the relationship.	**Love your neighbour as yourself** – it is unkind to expect that they can all be equally important in a three-way relationship. Monogamous relationships are challenging enough.

Now test yourself

TESTED ☐

Which Bible verses do you know of that might suggest polyamory is not acceptable?

Apply your knowledge

Look at the example of Iker, Mina and Jax again. Identify which principles have been missed out. How do they help to show whether or not the act of polyamory is loving in their situation?

Exam checklist

Can you:
- define the following terms: homosexuality, polyamory
- state a brief scenario to work with
- apply the ten principles to your worked example
- show how the principles would bring about different outcomes
- use Bible references to back up your arguments?

Revision activity

Look in the news for a current story relating to homosexual or polyamorous relationships. Try to apply the principles of Situation Ethics to the story.

Issues for analysis and evaluation

There are six issues for analysis and evaluation listed on the specification as examples of the kinds of AO2 questions you could be asked. Consider the possible conclusions to the question before you establish lines of argument. Develop these lines of argument by giving examples or evidence to demonstrate the points.

The degree to which agape is the only intrinsic good

REVISED

Agape is the only intrinsic good	Agape is not intrinsically good	Agape is an intrinsic good but not the only one
1 Corinthians 13:13 is clear that agape is more important than any other characteristic.	Agape is too subjective to be considered intrinsically good.	In 1 Corinthians 13:13, other goods are mentioned: faith and hope.
Jesus states that the law is based upon the command to love God and your neighbour.	Some acts seem good without being loving, e.g. consider the Trolley Problem (see page 79).	Galatians 5:22–23 mentions joy, peace, patience, kindness, goodness, faithfulness and self-control.
Laws are useful only if they produce an outcome that is loving to people.	You can't love everyone, e.g. abortion is loving to the mother, but not to the child.	In Exodus, Abraham's obedience to God's commands is of primary importance.
To be treated with loving kindness and compassion is something everyone wants.	Agape is an over-simplification, there is more to morality than this.	Matthew 5:17 says that Jesus came to fulfil the law not abolish it.

Whether Fletcher's Situation Ethics promotes immoral behaviour

REVISED

It does promote immoral behaviour	It does not promote immoral behaviour	It allows immoral behaviour but does not promote it
Human desires are promoted as more important than God's commands.	Situation Ethics cannot promote immorality because the only moral thing is love.	It tries to do what is best but inadvertently leads to immorality.
It encourages people to reject God's commands if it suits them.	It follows Jesus' example, so it must be moral.	You can't love everyone equally, so it is too idealistic to be realistic.
Some actions are simply wrong, e.g. rape, but theoretically Situation Ethics could allow it.	It only requires law breaking when the situation is so extreme that the law fails.	It doesn't require people to murder but accepts that such acts are sometimes necessary.
Jesus never broke any of the ten commandments, only the pharisaic laws.	Manipulation of agape for selfish ends is a risk, but not advocated.	It allows us to choose between two bad options when that is all that is available.

The extent to which Situation Ethics promotes justice

It does promote justice	It does not promote justice	It promotes justice, but it does not achieve it
One of the six fundamental principles is that justice and love are the same thing.	The agapeistic calculus disregards the minority to bring love to the majority.	Justice is impossible. We can't show love to everyone even though Fletcher wants us to.
Personalism accepts that circumstances make it easier for some to obey rules.	Justice is equal treatment, not the same outcome. The same rules should apply to all.	Situation Ethics is idealistic but not realistic.
Justice is a fair outcome. People have diverse needs to reach the same goal.	It is impossible to legislate for Situation Ethics in a society, so it cannot promote justice.	Some people are resistant to help and so we cannot provide love if they don't want it.
Loving your neighbour means that we don't give preferential treatment to anyone.	It encourages a free choice of behaviour. This promotes anarchy, not justice.	It is not fair to the victims of crime to show equal love to criminals.

The effectiveness of Situation Ethics in dealing with ethical issues

REVISED

Situation Ethics is effective in dealing with ethical issues	Situation Ethics is ineffective in dealing with ethical issues	Situation Ethics is partially effective in dealing with ethical issues
It allows the individual autonomy to weigh up the situation for themselves.	It is not possible to judge the actions and laws of others because everything is relative.	Laws help govern society; agape is useful for the individual.
It is adaptable to new ethical scenarios that present themselves to society.	It allows actions that most others would recognise as intrinsically bad.	Agape combined with other factors (such as law) could regulate each other.
It can make allowances for extreme situations.	Laws are put in place for a reason, to prevent problems that have arisen historically.	It is beneficial to us all to make sure that laws are applied in a loving, compassionate way.
By not rejecting law entirely, it still provides structure to society.	We cannot know all the future consequences that will arise because of one decision.	Situation Ethics can address our attitude but cannot protect us from others' immoral acts.

Whether agape should replace religious rules

REVISED

Agape should replace religious rules	Agape should not replace religious rules at all	Agape should be taken alongside religious rules
Jesus set the precedent that we can put laws aside if it is loving to do so.	God's laws do not change, they are absolute ('I the Lord do not change' – Malachi 3:6 NRSV).	Agape is useful for individuals but cannot run a society.
The New Testament preaches freedom from the restrictions of Judaic Law.	Jesus said that he had not come to replace the law but to fulfil it.	Rules are useful for society to make sure vulnerable people are protected.
If we follow agape, then we will usually end up doing what the law suggests anyway.	Religious laws protect the vulnerable and preserve our relationship with God.	Agape is a useful personal ethic for when rules don't address the situation.
Focus on the law means we become like the Pharisees; Jesus preached against them.	Our reason is flawed; we cannot be trusted to know the best way to be loving.	Agape can ensure that the rules don't become too cold-hearted.

Issues for analysis and evaluation

The extent to which Situation Ethics provides a practical basis for making moral decisions for both religious believers and non-believers

It is practical for both believers and non-believers	It is impractical for both believers and non-believers	It is practical for believers but not for non-believers
While God is the basis, it is possible to be loving whether you are religious or not.	Humans are not omniscient; we cannot judge in advance what the loving ends might be.	Non-believers have no reason to be interested in the teachings of Christ.
The principle of positivism requires faith in love, not faith in God.	Love is too subjective for anyone to use it to judge behaviour.	Non-believers will prefer Utilitarianism, which does not resort to scripture.
A principle of Situation Ethics is pragmatism – practicality is written right into the theory.	Non-believers cannot view Jesus as a good role model without faith in his divinity.	Practical means useful – agape is not useful since the word is only meaningful to believers.
It requires use of reason to see how to best be loving, so anyone can apply it.	It is an impractical way to run a multi-cultural or secular society without proselytising.	Non-believers do not share the motivation to emulate God by following this theory.

Specimen exam questions

Sample AO1 questions

1 Outline the four working principles and the six fundamental principles of Situation Ethics. **(AS only)**
2 Compare Fletcher's Situation Ethics with the ethical approaches of legalism and antinomianism.
3 Examine how biblical teaching is used to support Situation Ethics.
4 Explain the teleological and consequentialist theory of Situation Ethics.
5 Apply Fletcher's Situation Ethics to the ethical issue of polyamorous relationships.

> **Revision tip**
> Read the trigger words carefully before answering a question. When your trigger word asks you to compare, you are expected to show the similarities and differences between two or more things.

Sample AO2 questions

1 Evaluate the view that agape is a better approach to ethics than religious laws.
2 'Situation Ethics promotes fair treatment for all people.' Evaluate this view.

> **Revision tip**
> An evaluation question is different from an AO1 question because it is asking you to weigh up a dilemma. Avoid lengthy, AO1-style descriptions in an AO2 answer.

3D Classical Utilitarianism –Jeremy Bentham's Act Utilitarianism: happiness as the basis of morality

Bentham's theory of 'utility' or 'usefulness'

REVISED

- Utilitarianism is a **secular** theory.
- It predates Bentham and can be traced back to the ancient Greeks, such as Plato and Epicurus.
- Bentham aimed to be rational, logical and scientific in his approach to moral behaviour.
- David Hume had called Utilitarianism the 'theory of usefulness'.
- Bentham's theory of usefulness considers how useful an action is. In other words, how practical is it?

Ultimate aim is to pursue pleasure and avoid pain

REVISED

- The desire for happiness or pleasure is universal.
- Everyone also wants to avoid pain.
- This is part of human nature and what we all have in common.
- These are the only things that can be used to determine the goodness or badness of an act.
- No act is intrinsically good or bad.
- A good act is directly related to how much happiness is produced by the outcome of the act.
- This is **hedonistic** in that it is concerned with pursuing pleasure.

Principle of utility

REVISED

Bentham was interested in constructing a system of law to approve or reject both individual behaviour and common legal systems that apply to the whole of society.

- His principle of utility is sometimes known as the greatest happiness for the greatest number.
- Francis Hutcheson had coined the term 'greatest happiness for the greatest number'.
- So, the principle of utility aims to promote maximum happiness for society.
- The society is the total of all individual members, so individual happiness is also vital.
- The greatest happiness need not always be for the majority; it can be for a minority if more happiness in total is achieved by an act.
- But individual happiness alone is not enough for Utilitarianism.
- Therefore, this is a democratic theory, not an egoistic one.
- When judging the goodness or badness of an act, we must weigh up the amount of overall happiness that will be caused.
- We must balance this against the overall amount of pain that will result.

Who was Jeremy Bentham?
Jeremy Bentham (1748–1832) was an English philosopher, economist, legal expert and social reformer. He proposed Classical Utilitarianism in his book *An Introduction to the Principles of Morals and Legislation*. Bentham was looking to address widespread social injustice and to avoid unnecessary suffering for the poor and vulnerable.

Typical mistake

Don't spend too long talking about Bentham's life history. The examiner is more interested in the ethical theory than Bentham's life.

Utilis – Latin, meaning useful.

Secular – non-religious.

Hedonism – the pursuit of pleasure.

Now test yourself

1 Which scholar is most associated with Classical Utilitarianism?
2 What did Hume call this kind of ethical theory?

TESTED

The hedonic calculus as a means of measuring pleasure in each unique moral situation

Bentham wanted to make the ethical calculations as scientific as possible. Consequently, he formulated the hedonic calculus, which should be applied to each situation without using any prefabricated rules. The **calculus** was intended to measure the quantity of pleasure or pain produced in any given act, to decide whether it is moral or not.

- The hedonic calculus is sometimes called the felicific calculus.
- 'Hedonic' comes from **hedone**, which is the ancient Greek word for pleasure.
- As we have established, Classical Utilitarianism is hedonistic, so it is concerned with happiness or pleasure as its end.
- Other Utilitarian theories may emphasise different sorts of ends (Situation Ethics or Christian Utilitarianism had the end of love).
- The hedonic calculus is an attempt to calculate the balance between the pleasure and pain that result from any action.
- Bentham felt that we can weigh up pleasure **quantitatively**.
- This meant he was more interested in how much happiness will occur and not concerned with the type of happiness or what kind of quality it has.
- All viable alternative courses of action should be measured in terms of the calculus.
- Bentham aimed to create a mathematical way of working out the quantity of pleasure produced by an act.
- He included seven criteria in his calculus:
  1 **D**uration – the amount of time that the happiness will last.
  2 **R**ichness – how much more happiness this act will lead to in the future (fecundity).
  3 **P**urity – how much the act will be contaminated by pain.
  4 **R**emoteness – how long we will have to wait until the happiness starts (propinquity).
  5 **I**ntensity – how strong the sensation of happiness will be.
  6 **C**ertainty – how sure we are that the happiness will occur.
  7 **E**xtent – how many other people the happiness will affect.
- He claimed that pleasure and pain can be measured in the same way as anything else. A unit of pleasure was called a hedon, a unit of pain was called a dolor.

> **Calculus** – mathematical method of determining the amount of something.
>
> **Hedone** – ancient Greek word for pleasure.
>
> **Quantitative** – concerns the quantity or amount of happiness gained.

> **Revision tip**
>
> The acronym **DR PRICE** can help you to remember all seven of the different elements of the calculus.

'Prejudice apart, the game of pushpin is of equal value with the arts and sciences of music and poetry.' [pushpin is as good as poetry]
Bentham, J. (1825) *The Rationale of Reward*. London: John and H.L. Hunt, p. 206

Now test yourself

1 Write out the acronym DR PRICE.
2 Shut the book and write out all the distinctive features of the hedonic calculus based on this acronym.
3 Can you now define each one?

> **Typical mistake**
>
> Avoid using the same words, or very similar ones, to define key terms. To say that purity means how pure the pleasure is does not show the examiner that you understand the meaning of the term.

Act Utilitarianism

- Act Utilitarianism is a term that is applied retrospectively to Bentham. This means that we associate it with him, not that he created the term.
- Act Utilitarianism weighs up each individual act according to the situation in which it occurs.
- No rules are applied in advance.
- No attempt is made to look historically at the results of prior actions and formulate any kind of precedent.
- Each situation is unique and should be weighed up according to the hedonic calculus.

Act Utilitarianism is:

Relativistic

- There are no absolutes, no rules formulated in advance.
- No act is intrinsically good or bad.
- The goodness or badness of an act is all relative to how much happiness is caused.
- A bad act is bad only if it produces more pain than happiness.

Consequentialist

- All acts are assessed according to the possible outcome or result of the act.
- The principle of certainty from the hedonic calculus means we must consider how sure we are that the potential consequences will happen.

Teleological

- Telos is the Greek word for goal or end.
- The goal of any act is to produce maximum happiness.
- The end justifies the means. This means that it doesn't matter what act you perform as long as the most possible happiness is produced.
- The goal of all moral actions is to produce happiness and avoid pain.

> **Revision activity**
>
> 1 From your favourite TV programme, choose a dilemma that some of the characters are facing and apply the seven areas of the hedonic calculus to it.
> 2 Make a list of the difficulties that you faced when doing this – they might be good lines of argument for analysis and evaluation.

> **Apply your knowledge**
>
> The Trolley Problem was posed by Philippa Foot in 1967. The thought experiment states that you are the driver of a trolley which rounds a bend to reveal five workmen on the track. You must apply the brakes to prevent a collision, but they fail to work. You can turn the trolley to a side track, but there is one workman on that line too. No one can get out of the way in time.
> - Apply Bentham's version of the utility principle to this problem.
> - Use his hedonic calculus.
> - What kind of difficulties do you see?
> - Does it make a difference if you know the side track workman?
> - Does it make a difference if you are an observer rather than a driver and instead of diverting the trolley, you can derail it by pushing one person in front of the trolley, thus killing that person but saving the five?

> **Now test yourself**
>
> 1 Why would Utilitarianism be considered relativistic?
> 2 Explain what Act Utilitarianism is.
>

> ## Exam checklist
>
> Can you:
> - name the person credited with developing Classical Utilitarianism
> - explain the ultimate aim of Utilitarianism
> - state the utility principle
> - define the following terms: utility, hedonism, intensity, duration, certainty, remoteness, fecundity, purity, extent, relativism, consequentialist, teleological
> - detail the content of the hedonic calculus
> - understand and accurately use terms like quantitative, secular and calculus
> - explain the key features of Act Utilitarianism?

3E John Stuart Mill's development of Utilitarianism: types of pleasure, the harm principle and the use of rules

Who was John Stuart Mill?

John Stuart Mill (1806–1873) was the son of philosopher James Mill and the godson and pupil of Jeremy Bentham. He was a philosopher, political economist and one of the first members of parliament to call for women's suffrage. In his books *Utilitarianism* and *On Liberty*, he explains his development of Bentham's version.

Challenging Utilitarianism

A common challenge used against Utilitarianism is the sadistic guards problem.

There is an innocent man, wrongly imprisoned, being watched over by three sadistic guards who gain pleasure through torturing their charge. According to Bentham's quantitative version of Utilitarianism, Mill argues that the torture is allowable because there is more pleasure than pain being produced by this act. Yet most of us would argue that the act is surely wrong.

Mill's idea that not all pleasure is the same

REVISED

A notable change made by Mill to Bentham's Utilitarianism was to focus on the claim that pleasure was **qualitative** instead of quantitative.

- Thomas Carlyle had called Utilitarianism 'pig philosophy' because it appealed to basic, animalistic urges rather than more sophisticated human requirements.
- Mill agreed that what makes us human is that we want more out of life than the basic swinish pleasures.
- Mill interpreted pleasure like Aristotle. Eudaemonia is the kind of happiness that we all seek.
- Mill claimed that pleasure could be analysed qualitatively. So, there are pleasures that could be deemed as higher pleasures and some that are lower.
- Higher pleasures are of greater value than lower pleasures.

> **Qualitative** – relating to the standard or worth of pleasure achieved.

> **Higher pleasure** – intellectual, what makes us human rather than like other animals, superior to other pleasures.
> E.g. Reading a book, engaging in philosophy, scientific study, visiting an art gallery, spirituality.
> **Lower pleasures** – basic, physical, animalistic.
> E.g. Eating, drinking, sleeping, sex.

- We must satisfy lower pleasures to exist, but higher pleasure can be worth sacrificing a lower pleasure for.
- When we make a moral decision, we should weigh up the value of the act based on whether there is a higher quality pleasure at stake or a lower quality one.

- We don't always choose the higher pleasure over the lower one if we haven't been educated and experienced the full range of pleasures properly.
- So, everyone should be exposed to the higher pleasures through education as it helps them to make better moral choices.

In the example of the sadistic guards, the kind of pleasure that the guards gain is very base and does not outweigh the severe pain experienced by the one prisoner, even though there are more of them. Therefore, the act of torture is not justified.

> 'It is better to be a human being dissatisfied than a pig satisfied. It is better to be Socrates dissatisfied than a fool satisfied.'
>
> Mill, J.S. (1863) *Utilitarianism*. London: Parker, Son and Bourn, West Strand, p. 14

Now test yourself

TESTED

1 What kinds of happiness did Mill feel would be more important?
2 How do we choose between different types of happiness?
3 Why did Mill and Carlyle think Bentham's Utilitarianism was animalistic?

The harm principle

REVISED

Mill valued individual freedom or liberty. To protect happiness, it is vital that the individual has the right to make decisions about their own life. However, sometimes pursuit of happiness can interfere with the happiness of others.

The harm principle is a rule created to solve this dilemma. It states that we may never limit the freedom of others to act, except to prevent harm being done to other people.

Other than to prevent harm to others, and *only* to prevent harm to others, the individual should have complete freedom to make their decisions and have sovereignty over their own lives and bodies. This is the case even if they wish to cause harm to themselves.

There are some exceptions to this freedom:
- a child (someone who doesn't know any better)
- someone with mental health difficulties that make it difficult to judge for themselves
- someone without sufficient good education (e.g. from Mill's view – backward societies).

In these cases, we may need to interfere with personal liberty.

In the instance of the sadistic guards, the torture of the prisoner is not acceptable. The guards cannot harm another person just to achieve majority happiness. While they may be free to torture each other if they all wish to participate, the prisoner is an unwilling victim and so is protected.

Rule Utilitarianism

REVISED

Building on Aristotle's work, Mill argued that Utilitarianism is about maximising happiness in the form of Eudaemonia. If we promote society's well-being, it will support our individual happiness. For a happy society, the well-being of individuals needs to be considered. This means that we must develop rules that make it a duty for society to care for the individuals within it.

- Historically, there are rules that have been established that will always lead to happiness regardless of the situation.
- Not all actions need to be morally assessed as they are right if they conform to a historical rule that has demonstrated that it fulfils the principle of utility.
- The harm principle is one of these rules that have been set for all circumstances.
- What is right and wrong for one person is right and wrong for all.
- As a result, Mill's version is retrospectively called **Rule Utilitarianism**.

> There are two versions of Rule Utilitarianism (weak and strong):
> **Strong rule** – once the rules are set, they cannot be broken under any circumstances.
> **Weak rule** – rules can be broken if necessary to establish maximum happiness in an extreme situation.

John Stuart Mill's version tends to be classified as weak rule because he accepted that there were times when rules may need to be set aside to achieve greatest happiness for the greatest number.

In the sadistic guards example, a rule that will enhance the general well-being of society could be that the torture of prisoners is never allowed. This would encourage individuals to flourish without fear and thus society will prosper.

> **Rule Utilitarianism** – applying the utility principle to a general issue that will generate a rule to promote happiness. This rule will then be applied to all individual situations.

> **Typical mistake**
>
> Students often conflate Rule Utilitarianism with the qualitative measure that Mill put in place. When defining Rule Utilitarianism, you should not include a consideration of quality of pleasure. Mill was interested in both but they are two separate issues.

Now test yourself

TESTED

1 Close this book and then write out the harm principle. Open the book and check your answer.
2 Give three reasons why Mill would not allow the sadistic guards to torture the innocent prisoner.

> **Revision tip**
>
> You could prepare an example of a rule in advance of the exam concerning the keeping of a promise. You could also consider whether it works best as a weak or strong rule.

Mill's Utilitarianism as a teleological/ deontological hybrid

REVISED

Mill's version of Utilitarianism is not so clearly teleological.

- It is teleological in the sense that when establishing a rule, this is done through considering the goal of happiness or pleasure for the majority in general.
- In weak Rule Utilitarianism, a rule may be broken if it doesn't achieve the utility principle in a particular instance.
- It is deontological because once a rule is established, it becomes a duty for us to uphold this law for the sake of majority happiness.
- The strong Rule Utilitarian may never break this rule.

Exam checklist

Can you:
● state the problem that occurs with Bentham's version of Utilitarianism
● explain Mill's distinct types of pleasure
● give examples of pleasures that are higher or lower
● state the harm principle
● explain how this can be used to benefit individuals and society
● define what is meant by Rule Utilitarianism
● explain the difference between weak and strong rule
● define teleological and deontological ethics
● explain how Mill fused both in his Utilitarianism
● give an example to demonstrate how Mill's Utilitarianism might be applied?

3F Bentham's Act Utilitarianism and Mill's Rule Utilitarianism – application of the theory

The application of Utilitarianism to animal experimentation is exceedingly complex. It is unclear, for example, whether we should consider the individual animal, the specific piece of research or the human that will benefit.

The application of Bentham's Act Utilitarianism to animal experimentation for medical research

Animal experimentation refers to the use of animals to learn how to medically treat humans. It can include the following:
- **dissecting** animals to discover how they function or the effect of an illness/drug on their bodies
- **vivisection** or surgery on live animals for experimentation, research and training
- treating animals with experimental drugs to check their safety for human use
- imposing injury or disease upon animals to observe their effects and learn from them
- rearing animals and keeping them specifically for testing on them in a lab.

It includes the use of a variety of animals that are closest to human physiology or the easiest to experiment with – for example, mice, rats, dogs, pigs, rabbits and primates.

> **Dissection** – taking a body apart to analyse its internal structure.
>
> **Vivisection** – operating on live animals for experimental purposes.
>
> **The unsuperable line** – the benchmark by which we judge how we treat other beings.

What would Bentham say?

Bentham considered an animal's capacity for suffering to be **the unsuperable line** that takes priority over their capacity for reason or language. The hedonic calculus is applied to achieve the maximum quantity of happiness, but no general rules or precedent for action about animal testing can be created.

> 'The question is not, can they reason? Nor, can they talk? But can they suffer?'
> Bentham J. (1780) *Introduction to the Principles of Morals and Legislation.* Oxford: Clarendon Press, Chapter 17

Is animal experimentation ethically acceptable?

> **Bill and Spider the Pig**
> Bill has a congenital heart defect. He is 13 years old and in heart failure. The only current option is a heart transplant but there are not enough human hearts. Research into **xenotransplantation** could save Bill and others like him. Spider and other pigs would die in the testing and transplant process. (See the top of the next page for the application table for this example.)

> **Xenotransplantation** – using genetically altered animal organs, bred for transplant into other species.

	Bill and Spider
Yes	**Duration:** ● Bill is young and has years of life in front of him. ● Spider and other pigs would be slaughtered and thus free from pain. **Extent:** ● Bill's parents, siblings and friends are all affected. ● Spider does not have a piggy family to miss him or worry for him. **Richness:** ● Bill would have a capacity for increasing happiness as he lived his life normally. ● Spider's sacrifice would enable others to have the same treatment.
No	**Extent:** ● Millions of animals will be reared for testing and then for the procedure. ● Bill's family and friends will live on regardless of Bill's treatment. **Richness:** ● Animal experimentation is unreliable, leading to minimal future happiness. ● Bill will not be helped directly, since it is time-consuming to develop treatment. **Purity:** ● The pleasure gained by treating Bill is contaminated by pain for Spider. ● Many other animals have suffered for this process to be developed.

Revision tip

You may not have time to elaborate on every point of the hedonic calculus. Prepare to demonstrate depth with a few of the best points.

Typical mistake

Students sometimes don't answer the question carefully enough. To apply Utilitarianism to animal testing is not the same as describing testing methods or listing general arguments.

The application of Mill's Rule Utilitarianism to animal experimentation for medical research

REVISED

What would Mill say?

Mill argued that it was important to be able to empathise with the pleasure or pain experienced by animals. He grouped animals together with children, who need care from us since they cannot care for themselves. Mill valued some kinds of pleasure as lower in quality because they are animalistic, but this is only a feature of Mill, not of Rule Utilitarianism in general.

What rule could be formulated and applied regarding testing on animals to research cancer treatment in humans?

Yes – animals can be tested on to research human cancer treatment	No – animals cannot be tested on to research human cancer treatment
● Animal testing leads to the human pursuit of pleasures after treatment. ● We should exercise our power to protect sick people from harm by testing. ● It has been used since ancient Greece to improve medical understanding.	● Pleasure is being experienced by humans, at the expense of animals. ● Vivisection violates the harm principle – methods are unnecessarily cruel. ● Animal testing only tells us more about animal physiology, not about human treatment.

Now test yourself
TESTED

1 Give three reasons why Bentham's hedonic calculus would reject animal testing.
2 Make a list of higher pleasures that only humans can experience.
3 Give two Utilitarian reasons to support a law for using animals in medical research.

The application of Bentham's Act Utilitarianism to the use of nuclear weapons as a deterrent

Deterrence theory says that belligerent countries are less likely to attack a country with a substantial nuclear arsenal at its fingertips. To be credible, it should always be prepared but never used. The worries about deterrence include:

- the cost of keeping, improving and maintaining competitive weapons
- the risk of accident/unauthorised use/misjudgement
- the environmental risk through testing
- the damage that would be done if such weapons were detonated.

What would Bentham say?

When applying Bentham, we must consider the utility principle quantitatively and not formulate any rules to use in other situations. We should apply the hedonic calculus to the unique situation. Bentham lived at a time before the development of nuclear weapons so does not comment directly on this issue.

> **Deterrence theory** – possessing nuclear weapons will dissuade an enemy from initiating an attack or acting against the desires of the armed country.
>
> **WMDs** – weapons of mass destruction (such as nuclear weapons) which can cause widespread destruction to humanity and their living environment.

Nine countries possess nuclear weapons intended to deter other nations from attacking them. Is this justified by Bentham's Utilitarianism?

Duration	• Hiroshima and Nagasaki showed it would shorten any conflict considerably. • Nuclear fallout and long-term consequences would be extensive.
Richness	• Possessing weapons leads to a climate of fear and mistrust between countries. • Such weapons kill indiscriminately, which would not lead to future happiness.
Purity	• Weapons would be used only in proportion to the threat by an enemy. • There are no geographical boundaries to the devastation caused by use.
Remoteness	• Pain experienced by detonating such weapons is far into the future. • Happiness is postponed by continual striving to develop superior weapons.
Intensity	• Survivors of an attack would experience severe pain for a lifetime. • The fear experienced by vulnerable, unprotected nations would be strong.
Certainty	• Animosity will increase between nations, escalating the threat of attack. • Activating such weapons will cause widespread destruction and genocide.
Extent	• Possession of such weapons ensures safety from threats by other nations too. • Possession of **WMDs** by competing countries has triggered wars in the past.

Now test yourself

1 Use three elements of the hedonic calculus to explain why the possession of nuclear weapons is morally acceptable.
2 Use a different three criteria of the calculus and explain why possession of nuclear weapons is unacceptable.

The application of Mill's Rule Utilitarianism to the use of nuclear weapons as a deterrent

What would Mill say?

We should establish the best thing to do generally between all countries. We must consider the harm principle and establish rules. We may also consider what will lead to higher pleasures when it helps to formulate a rule. Remember that Mill lived at a time before the development of nuclear weapons.

> What rule could be formulated and applied regarding the ownership and development of nuclear weapons as a deterrent?

Yes – a nation can morally own and develop nuclear weapons	No – a nation cannot morally own and develop nuclear weapons
● The greatest happiness for the majority is achieved if a nation feels equipped to defend itself in an emergency. ● Nuclear development fulfils the harm principle as they would be deployed only to protect the majority from further harm. ● Deployment of such weapons would be a last resort so by definition would create more happiness than an alternative.	● The greatest happiness for the majority is not achieved by making all other nations feel fearful or threatened. ● Detonation of such weapons violates the harm principle that power is exercised over others to prevent harm, not cause it. ● The cost of keeping and developing such weapons prevents development of other pursuits beneficial to human happiness.

Revision activity

Develop the table above and add three more arguments for each side.

You could consider:
- the consequences of disarming countries like the UK, USA, North Korea, Russia, France, China, India, Pakistan and Israel
- the value in political statements of threat
- the jobs that such a programme creates
- the environmental impact of testing weapons.

Apply your knowledge

Create a series of tweets each consisting of 280 characters between Bentham and Mill discussing whether the UK should continue to develop **Trident**. Consider the process they will use to decide, as well as whether they will agree on the outcome.

> **Trident** – Britain's nuclear weapon deterrent. It consists of four vanguard class submarines, each carrying 16 missiles. Each missile has eight nuclear warheads.

Exam checklist

Can you:
- list the key features of Bentham's Act Utilitarianism and Mill's Rule Utilitarianism
- define the technical vocabulary around animal testing and nuclear weapons
- state the main arguments of each scholar for and against animal testing
- state the main arguments of each scholar for and against the possession of nuclear weapons as a deterrent
- weigh up the strengths and weaknesses of each set of arguments
- give reasons why some arguments are stronger than others
- use an example to demonstrate your arguments?

Issues for analysis and evaluation

There are six issues for analysis and evaluation listed on the specification as examples of the kinds of AO2 questions you could be asked. Consider the possible conclusions to the question before you establish lines of argument. Develop these lines of argument by giving examples or evidence to demonstrate the points.

The degree to which pleasure can be seen as the sole intrinsic good

REVISED

Happiness is the sole intrinsic good	Happiness is not the sole good; there are other goods	Happiness is not intrinsically good at all
Happiness is universal; it is the only motivation for action.	There are other important things that we would give up our happiness to achieve.	Simply desiring happiness doesn't make it good.
Happiness is not dependent upon culture or religion. Anyone can seek it.	Love is more vital because it allows us to sacrifice our happiness for others.	If happiness is our goal, we risk sacrificing others for our own enjoyment.
Happiness is not restricted to human activity. All living beings require it.	Single principle ethics don't recognise the breadth and depth of human action.	Happiness is too subjective to be used as a measuring rod for human action.
Even religion aims to produce happiness for its followers.	Other prima facie principles could include consent or personal autonomy.	Objectively good things would be good regardless of personal feeling or preference.

The extent to which Act and/or Rule Utilitarianism work in contemporary society

REVISED

Act/Rule Utilitarianism works in modern society	Act/Rule Utilitarianism does not work in modern society	Act/Rule Utilitarianism works to some extent
Utilitarianism has influenced modern laws, e.g. medical treatment and poverty.	Act Utilitarianism is too complex to legislate in issues like drug addiction.	Act Utilitarianism does not accept a duty to prioritise anyone.
Rule Utilitarianism preserves modern values of autonomy and protects the vulnerable.	Rule Utilitarianism cannot protect the environment by considering human happiness.	Rule Utilitarianism protects the vulnerable, unless they are vulnerable to themselves.
Act Utilitarianism can flexibly manage complex modern dilemmas like animal rights.	Rule Utilitarianism is too rigid; modern society desires freedom from constraint.	Rules help us co-ordinate many people but never suit everyone's needs.
It is the only practical option for medical treatment when there are limited resources.	It is impossible to weigh happiness for humans, let alone animals.	Modern society needs control for health and safety legislation and human rights.

The extent to which Rule Utilitarianism provides a better basis for making moral decisions than Act Utilitarianism

REVISED

Rule is a better basis for moral decision-making than Act	Act is a better basis for moral decision-making than Rule	Act and Rule are both as good/bad as each other
Rule Utilitarianism will help to make faster decisions since it allows prefabricated rules.	Act Utilitarianism recognises the need for human autonomy in ethical decision-making.	Both appreciate the Golden Rule of treating others the way you wish to be treated.
Rule offers protection to the weak and vulnerable through the harm principle.	Act Utilitarianism is more flexible, since every dilemma is unique to that situation.	Both allow some personal autonomy weighed against the outcome for other people.
We live among other people and Rule recognises our duty towards their happiness too.	The hedonic calculus ensures a problem is considered from every angle.	Both wrongly assume we can measure happiness and pain as though they are objective.
It is easier to legislate, and to offer reward and punishment, if society has common rules.	Act Utilitarianism does not sacrifice happiness for the sake of a prefabricated rule.	Neither theory includes any reference to a higher objective authority, such as God.

Whether Utilitarianism promotes immoral behaviour

REVISED

Utilitarianism promotes immoral behaviour	Utilitarianism does not promote immoral behaviour	It allows immoral behaviour but doesn't promote it
Utilitarianism rejects the idea of objectively good, God-given laws.	The definition of moral behaviour is to promote maximum happiness.	Utilitarianism aims for a happy society but inadvertently allows minority suffering.
Act's promotion of base pleasures leads to heinous acts like torture of minorities.	Utilitarianism does not discriminate based on gender, race, social status or ability.	Bentham and Mill resisted slavery and sexism, yet the theory can allow these things.
Relativist theories force us to tolerate intolerable behaviour by not recognising absolutes.	Utilitarianism makes useful decisions. Impractical moral rules are useless.	The flexibility of Utilitarianism allows any act despite the noble aim of happiness.
Personal happiness is too subjective to be allowed to rule our behaviour.	Empathy is used to imagine others' pleasure or pain in our moral decision-making.	The Trolley Problem demonstrates that the utility principle is too simplistic.

The extent to which Utilitarianism promotes justice

REVISED

Utilitarianism promotes justice	Utilitarianism does not promote justice	Utilitarianism promotes justice but cannot achieve it
The utility principle is applied equally to all, regardless of background or situation.	Any theory that, in principle, allows acts like murder or rape for a 'greater good' is not just.	Utilitarianism is too idealistic. A suffering minority is not a fair price to pay.
The flexibility of Utilitarianism means that people's needs are prioritised above rules.	There is no rule in Utilitarianism that insists on fair treatment for all.	Justice is not synonymous with happiness. Punishing a criminal is fair, not pleasurable.

Utilitarianism promotes justice	Utilitarianism does not promote justice	Utilitarianism promotes justice but cannot achieve it
Mill and Bentham were both champions of social justice for all.	Utilitarianism is too subjective. There is no fair way of judging a fair share of happiness.	Everyone is treated equally in the deliberation process, but some are then cast aside.
Utilitarianism includes non-human animals in the evaluation process.	It values the act that produces the most happiness, not an act that shares it out evenly.	We tend to consider justice or fair treatment to be objective, while happiness is subjective.

The extent to which Utilitarianism provides a practical basis for making moral decisions for both religious believers and non-believers

REVISED

Utilitarianism is a practical basis for both believers and non-believers	Utilitarianism is not a practical basis for believers or non-believers	Utilitarianism is practical for non-believers but not believers
The utility principle is universal regardless of whether someone is religious.	Act Utilitarianism is impractical because it doesn't learn from previous experiences.	A non-believer has no better basis for moral decisions, but the believer has God.
Mill claimed that the utility principle is the godliest as it is equivalent to the Golden Rule.	Too much time could be taken up in emergency situations with lengthy deliberations.	Believers can never be content with relying on flawed human desires over the will of God.
It is also the aim of the ten commandments to create as much happiness as possible.	People value the happiness of key individuals over others, e.g. their spouse.	Utilitarianism approaches morality scientifically but believers prefer faith.
There is no direct reference to God, so it is inclusive but adaptable to any world view.	God's will is of greater importance to a believer than the happiness of humans.	Utilitarianism allows behaviour that is often condemned in religious texts.

Specimen exam questions

Sample A01 questions

1 Outline Bentham's hedonic calculus. **(AS only)**
2 Compare Act and Rule Utilitarianism.
3 Examine Mill's development of Utilitarianism as a deontological/ teleological hybrid.
4 Explain why Mill developed the idea that not all pleasures are the same.
5 Apply Bentham's Act Utilitarianism to the use of nuclear weapons as a deterrent.

Sample A02 questions

1 Evaluate the view that the harm principle works well in modern society.
2 'A religious believer could never follow a Utilitarian ethic.' Evaluate this view.

> **Revision tip**
>
> An 'Examine' question requires a detailed account of a complex issue. It is an A01 response, so does not require evaluation.

> **Revision tip**
>
> It is useful to be able to list arguments for and against a question. However, in an essay, you need to engage with the material. Weigh up which viewpoint seems to be the strongest by giving reasoning and evidence.

Theme 4 Determinism and free will

The materials contained in Themes 4A–F should be studied together, since they all impact upon each other. You should expect analysis and evaluation questions to require you to draw on knowledge from the whole theme.

4A Religious concepts of predestination

St Augustine

REVISED

Augustine was influenced by the work of Pelagius, who preached that humans have freedom to turn to God by themselves. Augustine's theology of predestination was a response to this challenge to God's omnipotence.

Doctrine of Original Sin

- In the beginning Adam and Eve, the first humans, were created perfect.
- They were given only one command – not to eat of the tree of knowledge.
- Adam chose to eat of the tree, against God's command.
- This was the first sin.

Role of concupiscence

- Original sin was committed at Eden through **concupiscence**.
- We were all seminally present in Adam so we all share in his guilt.
- Original sin is passed on through sex.
- Only Jesus didn't inherit Adam's sin, as he was born of a virgin.

Humanity as a 'lump of sin'

- We all deserve to be punished.
- We are massa peccati (a lump/mass of sin).
- We are so hopelessly corrupt that we can only sin.
- Our free will is wasted by desire to only sin.

An essential 'free' human nature

- Before the fall, Adam had free will and could have abstained from sin.
- Our essential human nature is free (liberum arbitrium).
- This was the way we were created by God in the beginning.
- We are still responsible for our own decisions.

Typical mistake

Don't conflate religious concepts of predestination with the philosophical concept of hard determinism. Religious concepts include the involvement of a superior being who predetermines an outcome. Philosophical concepts point to material causes.

Who was St Augustine?
St Augustine of Hippo (354–430) was bishop of Hippo in North Africa. His most important works are *The City of God* and *Confessions*. His theology was hugely influential on medieval Church thinking and modern western Christianity.

Concupiscence – intense longing directed away from God and towards the world; characterised by sexual acts.

The loss of human liberty to our sinful nature

- We have lost our freedom (libertas) due to sin.
- Our second nature is sinful and overrides our essential human nature.
- We freely choose only to sin.
- We are free; otherwise there would be no moral exhortation in scripture.

God's grace and atonement for the elect

- We cannot perform good works without God's grace and Christ's atonement.
- God **elects** some to be saved. They are known as the **remnant**.
- Christ came into the world and died for the atonement of the elect, not the **reprobates**.

Elect – those chosen by God to receive eternal life.

Remnant – those who are left behind after God's judgement when the rest are destroyed.

Reprobate – a sinner who is predestined to damnation.

Now test yourself

TESTED

1 What is concupiscence?
2 What is Christ's role in Augustinian thinking?
3 Describe our human nature.

Typical mistake

It is common for students to think that Augustine rejected free will entirely. Make sure that you understand how free will is vital to Augustine's thinking.

Revision activity

Place each bullet point on a card and shuffle. Rearrange the points into a chronological or rational order. Group together all points that fall under the same subtitle. Check the results against this book.

John Calvin

REVISED

Calvin's belief in the absolute sovereignty of God gave rise to his acceptance of predestination. Without predestination, he claimed, no one would be saved.

Doctrine of Election

- Also known as the Doctrine of the Living Saints.
- God has absolute sovereignty over all things.
- Humans are predestined from eternity in all their choices.

The absolute power of God

- The fall of Adam was the result of an absolute and positive decree by God.
- God exercises his sovereignty by choosing who is saved and who is damned.
- God's predestination is both his foreknowledge and his active decree.

The corrupted nature of humans

- **Total depravity** means humans are tainted by sin in every way because of the fall.
- Humans are incapable of doing a good act apart from God's grace.
- We cannot choose God by ourselves.

Who was John Calvin?
Calvin (1509–1564) was a French reformer who wrote *Institutes of the Christian Religion*. His work was fundamental in the development of Calvinism, a protestant theology that broke from the tradition of the Roman Catholic Church.

Total depravity – every part of our nature is tainted by sin.

The elect and the reprobates

- Humans are not equal. Some are predetermined for election, others damnation.
- Eternal punishments or rewards are determined by God before birth.
- Called **Calvinistic fatalism** by some – we cannot choose good without God's grace.

Unconditional election

- We can be saved only through God's grace, not our works.
- God's grace allows some to have faith (**justification by faith**).
- This was decided before creation by God.

Limited atonement

- Christ's death atones for some people's sin but not all.
- **Particular redemption** means that salvation is limited to some, not that it is limited in power.
- It is a divine mystery who God will choose to be saved or damned (**double predestination**).

Irresistible grace and perseverance of the elect

- The reprobates are destined to suffer in eternal damnation no matter what they do.
- The elect yield to God's grace due to his power, not their virtue.
- They cannot commit **apostasy**.

> The Synod of Dort formed in 1618–1619 to settle the Calvinist dispute with Arminianism. Followers of Arminius (the Remonstrants) claimed we are free beings. Calvinists argued for:
> **T** – Total depravity
> **U** – Unconditional election
> **L** – Limited atonement
> **I** – Irresistible grace
> **P** – Perseverance of the saints

Apply your knowledge

1 Make a list of as many characteristics as possible of the theistic God.
2 Which of these characteristics are upheld by the theology of Augustine and Calvin?

Calvinistic fatalism – an accusation against Calvin that says all events are inevitable.

Justification by faith – humans are saved without reference to acts, only to faith.

Particular redemption – (limited atonement) only some people will be redeemed.

Double predestination – God predestines both the elect and the reprobates.

Apostasy – abandoning one's religion.

Revision tip

Use the acronym TULIP to help you remember Calvin's main points.

Now test yourself

1 Which scholar argued against Calvinism?
2 How are the elect chosen for eternal bliss?
3 What is double predestination?

TESTED ☐

4A Religious concepts of predestination

Exam checklist

Can you:
- define original sin, concupiscence and massa peccati
- explain our two human natures
- explain the relationship between free will and predestination for Augustine
- state Augustine's reasons for salvation
- define limited atonement, total depravity and unconditional election
- explain what is meant by double predestination
- state the reasons for salvation according to Calvin?

WJEC and Eduqas A level Religious Studies Religion and Ethics   93

4B Concepts of determinism

Hard determinism: philosophical

Hard determinism states that all human behaviour is caused by something external to us, so there are no free decisions. This is a **materialist** approach that operates according to the principle of **universal causation** – that every effect has an **antecedent** cause. This **incompatibilist** theory maintains free will to be illusory.

> **Who was John Locke?**
> John Locke (1632–1704) was an English empiricist philosopher and physician who studied at Oxford. He wrote *An Essay Concerning Human Understanding* (1690) and was an influential political thinker and writer.

Materialism – the only thing that exists is matter.

Universal causation – every event proceeds from another event without exception.

Antecedent – previous or pre-existing.

Incompatibilism – free will and determinism cannot be held to be true at the same time.

Free will is an illusion

Locke's thinking has been used to support the theory of universal causation. He claims that it is our ignorance of the causes of our actions that makes us think we are free.

He claims that to ask whether our will is free is a nonsense question. It is like asking whether your sight can hear. Freedom and will are both powers. We cannot ask whether one power has another power, but we can ask whether a person has a power. So, does a person have the power of freedom?

Man in bedroom illustration

Locke analyses the requirements for us to claim someone has the power of freedom. He concludes that a person must have:
- the power of thought
- the ability to act according to their thoughts.

He considers several examples:

A tennis ball	Cannot think
Man falling into water	Can think but not act according to thoughts
A person convulsively hitting another	Can think but not act according to thoughts

None of the above is free as they don't meet Locke's criteria.

> A sleeping man is carried into a room where there is a person with whom he longs to speak. The room is locked and when the man awakes, he decides to stay and talk to the person he has been wishing to see.

In the sleeping man example, the man can think, and act in accordance with his thoughts, so his action seems free. But his freedom is illusory.

The sleeping man illustration leads us to another question: Am I free to will what I will? The sleeping man, on awaking, desires to stay.
- For the desire to be free, it must be within his control.
- To be in his control, the desire must be formed by his will.
- That will must then be formed by his will to remain free.

- This leads to a logical regress.
- If it leads back to a first cause, external to the man, then he is not free.

Locke says that our action is preceded by our will, which comes from a desire for pleasure.

The sleeping man desires pleasure so decides to stay. Once he has decided to stay, provided no one forcibly evicts him, he will **necessarily** stay. His action is necessarily determined by his will.

Typical mistake

Not all scholars agree that Locke is a hard determinist. Ensure you know why some believe that he is, so that you can answer questions coherently.

Hard determinism: scientific

REVISED

Scientific determinism treats every feature of the world as mechanistic, so for every physical action there is a physical cause. This is the principle of universal causation.

Biological determinism – human behaviour is caused by an individual's genes

Biological determinism has its roots in the work of Darwinism and claims that all beings have a genetic formula. The discovery of DNA in 1953 by Watson and Crick and the mapping of the human genome in 2003 have given rise to the concept of **genetic fixity**.

Both physical and mental features are passed from parent to child at conception, meaning that all traits have a physical nature. In the study of genetics, some genes have been identified that are responsible for:
- religious experience
- sexuality
- addiction
- violence.

> While this idea dates back to ancient Greece, during the Second World War, the Nazi regime funded research into **eugenics**. This allowed scientists to research possibilities for eliminating some inherited characteristics and encouraging 'desirable' ones. This could take the form of forced sterilisation, genome editing or selective breeding. Such a view can lead to prejudice against race, gender, disability and sexuality.

Some scientists argue that such genes must be activated by certain features within a person's environment. Either way, this leads to the idea that we are not free but controlled by external factors.

Necessary – inevitable, fixed, certain.

Genetic fixity – all human behaviour is determined by genes inherited from parents.

Eugenics – Greek, meaning well-born; practices aimed at improving the genetic quality of a human population.

Hard determinism: psychological

REVISED

Who was Ivan Pavlov?
Pavlov (1839–1936) was a Russian psychologist known primarily for his work in **classical conditioning** techniques. He won the Nobel Prize in Physiology or Medicine in 1904 and he has been a major influence on the development of behavioural therapy.

Classical conditioning – a reaction that is trained through association.

Classical conditioning

Pavlov noticed that a natural reaction of a dog to food is to salivate and produce stomach acid. This reaction appears to be unconscious and not something that the dog wills. He discovered through experimentation that he could train such a response in a dog with the use of external stimuli.

Food – **unconditioned** stimulus	Dog salivates – unconditioned response
A bell is rung – **neutral** stimulus	Dog does not salivate – no response
Food + a bell is rung – **conditioning** stimulus	Dog salivates – unconditioned response
A bell is rung – **conditioned** stimulus	Dog salivates – conditioned response

The response of salivation would occur when there was neither sight nor smell of food and even when the dog was not hungry. This depends on the psychological mechanism of association. Pavlov's work led to developments from John Watson and later B.F. Skinner, who added rewards and punishments to speed up conditioning effectively (**operant conditioning**). If applied to human beings, it means that our behaviour is conditioned, rather than free.

Unconditioned – untrained.

Neutral – does not naturally cause a response.

Conditioning – training a specific behaviour.

Conditioned – trained.

Operant conditioning – behaviour controlled through reward and punishment.

Now test yourself

TESTED

1 What is hard determinism?
2 Why is John Locke considered by some to be a hard determinist?
3 Why would biological determinism suggest we are not free beings?

Revision tip

Ensure you can identify the features that make each approach deterministic. This is important in addressing questions on hard determinism.

Soft determinism: Thomas Hobbes

REVISED

Soft determinism, also known as **compatibilism**, accepts that both determinism and free will can simultaneously be true. Soft determinists propose that we possess only the **liberty of spontaneity**.

Who was Thomas Hobbes?
Hobbes (1588–1679) was an English philosopher and author of *Leviathan*. His social contract theory is seen to be the foundation of western political philosophy.

Compatibilism – the notion that free will and determinism can both be accepted without logical paradox.

Liberty of spontaneity – the ability to act as we choose without constraint.

Internal and external causes

There is no such thing as an agent whose action is uncaused, but there are different types of causes. Free will does not mean we are uncaused. It means we are free from constraint.

Every action has an antecedent cause and so both the above acts are necessarily caused. The one act that is unconstrained, originating from an internal cause, is free.

External cause	From outside the self
	A constraint of will
	Part of a causal chain
	Necessary
Internal cause	From within the self
	The will
	Part of a causal chain
	Necessary

A man throws his belongings into the sea because the boat lurches – external cause (not free).
A man throws his belongings into the sea because he is frightened that otherwise the boat will sink – internal cause of fear (free).

Soft determinism: A.J. Ayer

REVISED

Ayer offers us two options. Either:

1 An act is uncaused – such events are random accidents and so not free.
2 An act is caused – this leads us back to determinism.

Caused acts vs forced acts

Free will should not be contrasted with determinism. Instead it should be contrasted with force or constraint. All acts are clearly caused, not uncaused, but a forced or constrained act will be one that occurs regardless of a person's resolve. A free act is caused by the will of the agent.

Provided that:

1 there is a choice in how to act
2 I can act according to my own desires
3 I am not constrained/forced

I am acting freely. Being caused just provides an explanation for my actions.

> The kleptomaniac steals even if he resolves not to. He is constrained. The regular thief's action is caused by a lack of money or a desire for a thrill, but he is not constrained and if he decides not to steal, then he won't. One can act in accordance with his desires; the other cannot.

Now test yourself

TESTED

1 What is compatibilism?
2 What example does Hobbes give to demonstrate the difference between internal and external causes?
3 Why does Ayer say that there is a difference between cause and constraint?

Revision activity

There are many different examples used by the scholars in this section. Make a poster with pictures to represent each example. Place sticky notes with different facts about each theory around the correct examples.

Apply your knowledge

Consider the following scenario:

A mother of a one-year-old child calls the police and confesses to harming her daughter. When the police arrive, the child is dead and there is evidence that she has been shaken.

What would each of the five determinist approaches say regarding the mother's responsibility for her actions?

Exam checklist

Can you:
● define the terms hard determinism, soft determinism, compatibilism and incompatibilism
● explain the three hard determinist approaches
● explain both soft determinist approaches
● give examples to illustrate each approach
● identify the key differences between each approach?

4C The implications of predestination/determinism

The implications of determinism on moral responsibility

If external causes operate upon us in all our actions, this raises questions regarding whether we can be held accountable for our behaviour. Does it make sense to praise the actions of a person who gives to charity if they were conditioned to do so by behavioural programming? Is it reasonable to blame or punish a violent person if their behaviour is caused by a specific gene?

The worth of human ideas of rightness, wrongness and moral value

Human ideas of right and wrong are worthwhile	Human ideas of right and wrong are not worthwhile
Recognising the causes that operate upon us might help us redirect them. Concepts of right or wrong provide incentives to do so.	Philosophical determinism suggests our ideas of right and wrong are from prior causes. What I think is good never originates from me alone.
Ethical standards are not intrinsically worthy, but they help to keep society in order. This is valuable in its practicality. (Freud)	Ayer would argue such ideas are just a result of an emotional response, so are meaningless even if we act in accordance with our feelings.
Actions originating from an internal cause demonstrate the usefulness of a person's character as a member of society. (Hume)	We are conditioned to believe that some things are good and others bad. The conditioning stimulus is from family and society. (Freud)

The value in blaming moral agents for immoral acts

There is value in blaming moral agents	There is no value in blaming moral agents
Blaming is part of the conditioning stimulus needed to create a being who is useful to society. (Skinner)	A person's will is brought about by antecedent causes, so we might call it free, but it is more a consciousness of necessity. (Ayer)
Hobbes saw two purposes in punishment: 1 judging the value of an act 2 changing the behaviour of the agent.	The blame for any action, good or bad, lies prior to the agent who performs it. There is no sense in holding an agent morally responsible. (Darrow)
If an action is not forced, the agent can reasonably be blamed for their behaviour. (Ayer)	If an agent is violent because they have a gene predisposing them to this behaviour, blaming them will not affect their genetics.

Clarence Darrow, an American lawyer in the 1920s, successfully defended Nathan Leopold and Richard Loeb for the murder of Bobby Franks. They avoided the death penalty because, despite their privileged upbringing, they were not deemed responsible for the causes that operated upon them to make them behave in this way.

The usefulness of normative ethics

Normative ethics are not useful	Normative ethics are useful
If our behaviour is controlled by genes, then no normative ethics will ever change the way we act.	Any normative theory can operate as a conditioning factor upon people to ensure useful behaviour.
Normative ethics do not relate to any objective standard; they are formed because of societal programming. (Freud)	Normative standards are practical for the running of society but relate to no objective standard.
If we are not free, then we cannot be praised or blamed for following the rules. Therefore, they are meaningless.	If normative ethics are the result of an objective standard, then they operate as a cause that programs us anyway.

Typical mistake

Scholarly views can be interpreted in more than one way. Don't worry if you see that a scholar's views can be made to agree with both sides of a debate.

Revision tip

Identify which of the responses in the tables here come from hard determinists and which come from soft determinists.

Now test yourself

TESTED

1 Give three reasons why a hard determinist might reject the idea of moral responsibility.
2 Give three reasons why a soft determinist might reject moral responsibility.
3 Give three reasons why moral responsibility might be accepted by a determinist as reasonable.

The implications of predestination on religious belief

REVISED

If we are predestined by God, this means that our ultimate destination is controlled and decided by him without reference to our actions or choices at all. This has implications for the character of God and for the authority of scripture. The following is a set of responses that might be made to Calvinistic and Augustinian concepts of predestination.

The link between God and evil

If we are predestined, this leads to several possible conclusions regarding the link between God and evil:

Implications of Augustine	Implications of Calvin
God and evil are linked: • God created eternal damnation, suggesting that he planned for the fact that we would fall. • God is a passive excuser of evil by failing to elect some for heaven. • God is omniscient and so foreknew the evil humans would cause when he created us. • Allowing evil in the world to remain condemns millions to hopeless and pointless suffering.	**God and evil are linked:** • God is responsible for evil as he created all things. • God actively reprobated some, so he condemns them to hell regardless of their actions. • The elect are still sinful. God saves them anyway, apparently condoning evil deeds. • By predestining us, God performs evil acts, condemned by scripture (e.g. killing).
God and evil are not linked: • God did not make evil as he created only good things. • Humanity's essential nature was free, so it is our fault that we allowed evil to prevail. • God allows evil to stay so that we can understand good as something different.	**The link between God and evil is positive:** • God is benevolent, allowing the sinner to be forgiven through Christ and so saved from evil. • God's damnation of some is a divine mystery. We can trust in his authoritative judgement. • God is linked to evil through his rejection of it. By reprobating, he demonstrates his total power.

The implications for God's omnipotence and omnibenevolence

If we are predestined, this has an impact upon God's character:

Implications of Augustine	Implications of Calvin
God's character is limited: ● God cannot be all-loving if he elects only some to heaven and not all of us. ● God's power is limited if he sits back and allows us to be damned by the actions of Adam. ● God's power is limited if his creation can go wrong and become damaged.	**God's character is limited:** ● God is malevolent if he actively pre-reprobates people but still creates them anyway. ● God planned for evil and created it as part of the universe. He is powerful but evil. ● If God is all-loving but does not save us all, then maybe he lacks the power to do so.
God's character is unlimited: ● God remains uninfluenced by human activity. This means that he retains his power. ● God has provided salvation for the elect; no human action is necessary. ● God introduced no evil at creation and it was a perfect gift for humanity. He loves us.	**God's character is unlimited:** ● God is fully omnipotent because he controls all actions and outcomes. ● God is good and powerful because once we are predestined as the elect, we cannot fall away. ● Justice demanded human punishment. God did not have to save anyone, but he did out of love.

The use of prayer and the existence of miracles

Religious people believe:
● God answers the prayers of those who freely ask him for help
● God has the power to intervene in the natural course of events.

But this raises a few questions if we are predetermined.
● Do our prayers make any difference?
● If God controls our actions, is he making us pray?
● Why does God need miracles if he has everything planned out?
● If a miracle is a sign, what is its purpose if we can't choose how to respond?

Augustine	Calvin
Prayer is evidence that someone is faithful and thus one of the elect.	Prayer does not affect God or his preordained decisions regarding our destination.
We are incapable of good acts after the fall. It is God's grace that allows prayer, not free choice.	We cannot know whether God has elected or reprobated us. Prayer will not help us find out.
Prayer will not change God or his plans in any way.	This seems to contradict scripture, which tells believers to pray and God will hear them.
Christ's redemptive act on the cross is a miracle that was planned by God to save the elect.	If a miracle did occur, it would be because God ordained it, not because we prayed for it.
Miracles were planned in as part of God's created order when he created the world.	If God planned every aspect of creation, there is no need for interference through miracles.

Now test yourself

TESTED ☐

1 Who should be blamed for evil if we are predestined, and why?
2 Explain, with an example, why Augustine and Calvin might consider prayer to be useful.
3 Give three reasons why God might not be considered all-loving if we are predestined.

Revision activity

Revisit the problem of evil from Component 2: Philosophy of Religion. Make a list of all the areas of overlap within Augustine's theodicy and his view on predestination.

Apply your knowledge

There are many synoptic links to be made with other parts of the Ethics and the Philosophy papers.

Make a list of all the other areas where our being predestined or determined has an impact.

For example:
- the problem of evil – the free will defence
- Divine Command Theory – the meaningfulness of ethical language if we are not free.

Exam checklist

Can you explain why:
- human ideas of right and wrong might be worthless/useful if we are determined
- it might be useful/pointless to blame moral agents for their behaviour
- normative ethics have a place/are meaningless in a determined universe
- God might have some responsibility for the existence of evil if we are predestined
- God's qualities of omnibenevolence or omnipotence might be challenged/reinforced if he predestines us
- prayer and miracles might be deemed useless/still have a place in a predestined universe?

Issues for analysis and evaluation

There are six issues for analysis and evaluation listed on the specification as examples of the kinds of AO2 questions you could be asked. Consider the possible conclusions to the question before you establish lines of argument. Develop these lines of argument by giving examples or evidence to demonstrate the points.

A consideration of whether religious believers should accept predestination

REVISED

Religious believers should accept predestination	Religious believers should not accept predestination	Religious believers can logically accept both together
God is omnipotent only if he has control over all things, including human action.	God becomes the author of sin if he controls all human action.	Augustine manages to combine initial freedom and a fall to predestination.
There is evidence in scripture to support predestination (Romans 8:29).	Scripture gives us moral exhortations to persuade us to choose the good.	Genesis supports the idea that Adam and Eve began free and then fell to entrapment by sin.
The churches through history have accepted teaching on predestination, not freedom.	Church teaching is pointless if God predestines us because we cannot choose to respond.	Many churches and believers currently teach our freedom and God's power.
God's goodness can be seen in his salvation of the undeserving elect.	God is evil and life is futile if he has predestined some for hell regardless of their actions.	God's goodness is in his initial gift of freedom and his power in his forgiveness of the elect.

The extent to which God predestines humanity

REVISED

Humanity must be fully predestined by God	God has not predestined us at all; we are completely free	God's predestination of humanity is only partial
God is omnipotent and so must have power over everything.	God gave Adam and Eve a command which they disobeyed.	God planned a resolution to our mistakes, but the mistakes were fully our own.
For humans to be free gives them authority over God.	Human freedom requires only that God not act, not that his actions are overridden.	Single predestination means that God elects only some; he doesn't reprobate anyone.
Human fallibility demonstrates that they are incapable of any good action.	Complete freedom means the ability to make real choices, bad as well as good ones.	God knows the bad choices we will make but doesn't cause them himself.
God is the omniscient creator of all things. His nature requires complete authority.	God's nature as a judge requires human freedom to be worthy of judgement.	God has already judged our choices as he has seen them, but we performed them.

The extent to which philosophical, scientific and/or psychological determinism illustrate that humanity has no free will

Hard determinism makes freedom impossible	Hard determinism has not been irrefutably proven	Determinism is required for freedom to exist
No human act is independent of any outside influence, so action cannot be free.	Falsification says we need to find only one uncaused act to prove all determinism false.	Uncaused acts would be accidental or random. So, to be free, we must cause action.
The human genome shows our character traits and can predict our choices.	We know that other societal factors can switch genes on or off. Genes don't control all.	Sirigu's work shows that our brain contains a function to enable choice-making.
We make use of conditioning techniques in every aspect of childrearing.	Social conditioning happens but we can rebel against it. Teenagers do so all the time.	Conditioning simply provides a benchmark from which we can judge our own actions.
Even if action is a combination of genes and socialisation, we are still not free.	The human brain is so complex that some uncaused events may be possible.	Determinism just shows the reason for actions, not that they are out of our control.

Strengths and weaknesses of hard and/or soft determinism

REVISED

Hard determinism is strongest	Soft determinism is strongest	They are both equally powerful arguments
The evidence for hard determinism comes from every discipline.	Soft determinism combines evidence of causation with our experience of choice-making.	Or equally weak. Universal causation is not a necessary truth. It could be falsified.
Our shared human experience shows awareness of all the causes operating on us.	Shared experience is that we feel a sense of deliberation; internal causes make sense.	We cannot know all the interrelated causes for human action. Either could be true.
Religious arguments for God depend upon the belief in causality.	Or weakest, since there is no empirical evidence to support internal cause.	Causation is clearly correct, but it is unclear whether there are distinct types of causes.
The criminal justice system is dependent upon the existence of cause and effect.	Criminal justice makes sense only if we acknowledge responsibility from the agent.	Or equally weak. There is no point in punishment without complete responsibility.

Whether moral responsibility is an illusion

REVISED

Moral responsibility is completely illusory	Moral responsibility is necessary	We are completely responsible for all we do
Locke's sleeping man doesn't know he is locked in. He has no responsibility in staying.	Without moral responsibility, we are disabled because no choice matters.	The sleeping man is still responsible for his choice to stay in the room.
We cannot will what we will, so we cannot be ultimately responsible for what we will.	To reject moral responsibility means to reject social order and duty to each other.	Sartre sees us as tabula rasa, so we make ourselves and are therefore responsible.
Responsibility requires the ability to choose differently, yet external causes control us.	Moral responsibility requires causation so that we can be the cause of our actions.	Rogers says if we self-actualise and break free of conditioning, we become responsible.
Strawson says that we cannot choose our character so there can be no responsibility.	Smilansky sees it as a necessary illusion to ensure that we can act at all.	Our actions are caused by our own motive and character. It is this that makes us responsible.

Issues for analysis and evaluation

WJEC and Eduqas A level Religious Studies Religion and Ethics   103

The extent to which predestination influences our understanding of God

Predestination vitally affects our understanding of God	It does not matter if we are predestined or not	Free will influences our understanding of God more
God is believed to be omnipotent, so predestination is necessary.	God requires worship whether we are predestined or not.	God's gift of free will is more of a sign of his omnipotence.
God is the creator of everything in existence, which requires predestination.	A believer must act as though they are free to function, regardless of the reality.	God's role as judge after our death is dependent upon belief in free will.
This makes us see God as an arbitrary, partisan authority without mercy or compassion.	Faith in God is primary, and it must be a personal choice. We must assume we are free.	Free will is required for us to accept the meaningfulness of prayer for the believer.
God becomes the author of sin if we are predestined and so he is not worthy of worship.	God has created humans with the capacity to deliberate. The only choice is to use this.	Belief in the Holy Spirit as a guide is unnecessary if we have no free will.

Revision tip

There are more possible conclusions to some of the issues for analysis than have been explored above. Make a list of as many conclusions as you can, decide which you think is the strongest and support it with evidence.

Specimen exam questions

Sample AO1 questions

1 Compare the teachings on predestination from Calvin and Augustine.
2 Examine the concept of hard determinism.
3 Explain the implications of predestination on religious belief.
4 Compare the concepts of hard and soft determinism.
5 Examine the concept of soft determinism with reference to Hobbes and Ayer.

Sample AO2 questions

1 Evaluate the view that there is no value in blaming people for immoral action if determinism is correct.
2 'The strengths of soft determinism outweigh its weaknesses.' Evaluate this view.

Revision tip

Look to the materials on free will for ideas on how to challenge determinism.

4D Religious concepts of free will
Pelagius

REVISED

> **Who was Pelagius?**
> Pelagius (c. 354–418) was a British Celtic theologian thought by some to have been Irish. He was a highly educated **ascetic** and moved to work in Rome. He conflicted with Augustine on free will and most of his surviving works appear in the form of quotations from his adversary.

Ascetic – someone who follows a life of self-discipline and abstinence.

Orthodox – traditional Christian teaching.

The role of original sin

Pelagius is accused of denying the Doctrine of Original Sin as it seemed unfair to punish the whole of humanity for the sins of Adam and Eve. Pelagius is said to have claimed the following:
- Adam's sin only affected Adam.
- Even before the fall, Adam would have been subject to death.
- Human nature was modified but not corrupted by sin.
- Adam set a bad example, he did not condemn us.
- Christ set a good example, he did not save us.
- Children are born innocent of Adam's sin, in the same state as Adam before the fall.
- Baptism is not required for forgiveness of original sin, and children who die unbaptised can still go to heaven.
- Participation in a fallen world leads to sin, not inherited sinfulness.
- Rich baptised people will not inherit eternal life unless they give it all up.
- It is possible for some to die innocent if they never commit a sin, even before Christ.

Some of these accusations were apparently refuted by Pelagius in a letter to Augustine. Pelagius appears to deny these as they are contrary to **orthodox** Christian teaching.

Typical mistake

It is difficult to know the difference between what Pelagius said and what he is claimed to have said. There are almost no surviving works from Pelagius and the only records come from his opponents.

Humanity maturing in God's image and accepting the responsibility of free will

In Rome, Pelagius saw evidence of fatalistic immorality. If humans are justified by God's predestination and our actions do not matter, then moral behaviour has no purpose. Pelagius wanted humanity to take responsibility for their own sin, rather than passing the blame onto Adam, or God's will.

Pelagius is said to have argued:
- We are born with free will.
- We are born innocent.
- We are not mature enough yet to make good choices.
- We choose both good and bad acts.
- It is our action that makes us fit for salvation or condemnation, not faith alone.
- The fall enabled the possibility for humans to grow to maturity through learning to make good choices.
- The problems of sin are outweighed by the benefit of maturing into God's image.
- It is necessary for humans to make an effort to reject sin if they are truly repentant.

Free will as used to follow God's laws

We have a natural capacity to seek God. This is biblically evident through the gospels.

> 'Be perfect, therefore, as your heavenly Father is perfect.'
>
> Matthew 5:48 (NRSV)

Pelagius took this as a sign that God requires us to put effort into trying to act in a perfect way.

Scripture has God's law within it. Through the Law of Moses and the gospels we receive God's guidance, so that we can apply our free will and choose to follow his laws. We are saved by our acts, not simply by our faith alone.

The role of grace in salvation

Some accuse Pelagius of denying God's grace. However, Pelagius interprets grace differently from Augustine. God's grace will help humans achieve salvation but does not dictate it. Pelagian grace appears in three forms:

- **Original/natural grace** – given to all at birth. It is the natural, God-given gift of free will. Grace from God gives us the ability to do good if we choose to.
- **Grace of revelation** – given by God through reason and scripture. It is law or guidance, to inform us of God's will. We can then choose whether to obey.
- **The grace of pardon** – God's gift of forgiveness for us. This means that Christ's actions on the cross do not save us, but make forgiveness, if we seek it, possible.

Natural grace enables us to choose God for ourselves. It also means we can avoid sin and save ourselves. For Pelagius, we can be saved through works alone, and some understood this to mean that even the unbeliever, if they are without sin, has the potential to be saved.

In a letter to Pope Innocent I, Pelagius denied that he was a **heretic**, stating that we can do good works through free will but need divine help. All humans have this power of free will, but only Christians receive God's help through grace. Pelagius also denied that he rejected baptism of children for the forgiveness of sin. He was controversially **excommunicated** by Pope Zosimus in 418.

> **Heretic** – preaching contrary to orthodox Christian teaching.
>
> **Excommunicated** – officially excluded from the Church.

Predestination is God's foreknowledge, not his direction of our action. God knows in advance who will seek pardon and salvation for their sins but does not cause our salvation or damnation.

Now test yourself

TESTED

1 What did Pelagius say about the role of original sin?
2 Does it matter how we behave in this life?
3 What does Pelagius think grace is?

> **Revision tip**
>
> You cannot study Pelagius apart from Augustine. List the points of agreement and conflict between the two scholars.

Arminius

Denial of the Calvinist view of predestination

Arminius rejected Calvinistic predestination. He argued that this teaching made humanity automatons and God the author of sin. He amended his understanding of predestination rather than denying it, to allow room for both predestination and free will.

In his Declaration of Sentiments, delivered in 1608, Arminius defended his thinking:
1 Christ is the foundation and power behind salvation, reprobation is distance from him.
2 Election and reprobation are conditional upon human faith.
3 Election and reprobation occur with God's foreknowledge.
4 Grace is given by God but is utilised by humanity.

After Arminius' death, the Arminians systematised Arminius' thought into five articles of remonstrance and presented them against Calvinism at the Synod of Dort.

Article 1: conditional election

Predestination is God's foreknowledge (**middle knowledge**), not coercive power. God knows who will freely accept or reject Christ and rewards or condemns them accordingly as stated in scripture. This is decided by the omniscient God from the beginning of time based on what he foresees we will do.

> 'Whoever believes in the Son has eternal life; whoever disobeys the Son will not see life but must endure God's wrath.'
> John 3:36 (NRSV)

The effect of original sin on free will

Article 2: God's grace allows us to reject sin

Humanity is tainted by original sin. This deprives us of goodness, so we cannot choose God by ourselves. Free choice is possible only because the cross empowers us with the gift of grace to all, allowing us to freely choose Christ. Apostasy is possible, allowing us to freely turn away.

God's prevenient grace in allowing humans to exercise free will

Article 3: atonement requires Christ's assistance

Christ's death on the cross was for everyone. Through this, God has given us the Holy Spirit, who allows us to exercise our free will despite original sin. This gift of **prevenient grace** (or common grace) is given, regardless of any action of mankind. Nothing else is needed for salvation.

Typical mistake
Arminius was careful not to dismiss predestination outright but combined it with free will. The five articles of remonstrance attempted to show this thinking was orthodox and not heretical.

Conditional election – God foreknows but doesn't coerce our actions.

Middle knowledge – God's omniscience includes our possible actions as well as our actual choices.

Prevenient grace – (common grace) the gift of freedom to choose good, given through the Holy Spirit via Christ's death on the cross.

The elect and the possibility of rejecting God's grace

Article 4: resistible grace

Human freedom given by Christ's atonement is genuine; God plans to save everyone, but we can thwart his plans and be lost in hell. While we cannot choose God without his grace and power, that doesn't mean that we must choose him. The sinner chooses God; God does not force the sinner.

The election of believers being conditional on faith

Article 5: salvation requires our own efforts combined with God's assistance

Salvation depends on our own efforts in co-operation with God. We need, and should desire, God's assistance to strive against evil, but it is still our own effort. This gives people the protection of his grace not to be pulled away from him towards evil.

> 'I give them eternal life, and they will never perish. No one will snatch them out of my hand.'
>
> John 10:28 (NRSV)

Revision activity

Create a chart that lists the ways Arminius retains our free will on one side and all the ways he maintains God's authority on the other.

Now test yourself

TESTED

1 Who presented the five articles of remonstrance?
2 How does Arminius combine free will and predestination?

Apply your knowledge

1 Imagine your best friend must decide between going to a party or sitting down to revise. Can you say you know which (s)he will choose?
2 If you know, is (s)he free to choose it?
3 Is this example adequate to illustrate conditional election? Why/why not?

Exam checklist

Can you:
- explain Pelagius' thinking, including:
  - original sin
  - humanity maturing
  - human responsibility
  - the role of the law and grace
  - who Pelagius was refuting
- explain Arminius' thinking, including:
  - rejection of Calvinism
  - original sin
  - prevenient grace
  - resistible grace
  - conditional election?

Now test yourself answers at www.hoddereducation.co.uk/myrevisionnotesdownloads

4E Concepts of libertarianism

Libertarianism is a non-religious stance that asserts free decision-making. This philosophical position is incompatibilist since it claims our minds are unaffected by causation. Libertarians argue for both the **liberty of spontaneity** and the **liberty of indifference**.

Philosophical: Sartre

REVISED

> **Who was Jean Paul Sartre?**
> Sartre (1905–1980) was a French philosopher, writer and political activist. He is known for his contribution to existentialist philosophy in *Being and Nothingness* (1943).

Man is not free not to be free

As an existentialist, Sartre argued that humans make themselves.

- There is no God or objective dogma to guide us.
- Ethics and religion try to make rational sense of a senseless universe.
- The absurd universe is characterised by suffering and death.
- The agent alone is responsible for their decisions and actions.

Sartre said that existence precedes essence. Our identity is not fixed before we exist. We are born **tabula rasa**. This contradicts the Bible's claim that our soul pre-exists earthly life.

> 'Before I formed you in the womb I knew you.'
> Jeremiah 1:5 (NRSV)

Liberty of spontaneity – the ability to act as we choose without constraint.

Liberty of indifference – a being is uncaused in their actions, but still somehow responsible.

Tabula rasa – (Latin) a blank slate.

The gap – the distance between the operation of our minds and the physical world.

Bad faith – the adoption of false values (French: mauvaise fois).

We make ourselves from moment to moment, through free decision-making and action, evidenced by our self-conscious experience of deliberation before we act. There is no reason to assume that one decision is better than another.

There is a distance between the human mind and the external world (**the gap**). Cause and effect does not operate on our minds as it does on the world. We cannot override our physical restrictions, but being human involves freely forming our own ideals and taking responsibility for them.

- We make decisions and then act to bring about consequences.
- We see the consequences, then set our own ideals.
- We make further choices according to the ideals we invent.
- We are constantly aware we could choose differently.
- We thus make ourselves.
- This responsibility is a burden.
- We have no choice but to choose.

Waiter illustration

In claiming that our actions are caused by external influences, we deny our freedom and act in **bad faith**. This means we give in to social forces and adopt external values. We do this when the alternative of accepting responsibility in an absurd world is too painful for us. Sartre gives the illustration of a waiter:

> Imagine a pretentious waiter. His voice pompous, his actions ostentatious and overly keen. He is play acting as an automaton rather than a human. He knows deep down he is not purely a waiter; he is consciously deceiving himself.

The waiter acts in bad faith by denying his own freedom and adopting the role dictated by society. When we complain of our situations and how we are restricted by societal expectations, we act in bad faith. We are free to be authentically whatever we want to be.

Now test yourself

TESTED ☐

1 What does 'existence precedes essence' mean?
2 How do we make ourselves?
3 Why is freedom negative?

Scientific: Sirigu

REVISED ☐

Who is Angela Sirigu?
Angela Sirigu (1956–present day) is an Italian-born scientist whose training is in neuropsychology and **cognitive neuroscience**. She is based at the University of Lyon and is involved in applying a range of techniques to discover the functions of different brain regions.

Cognitive neuroscience – the scientific study of the biological processes that underlie mental action.

Parietal cortex – part of the brain that resides behind the frontal lobe at the back of the parietal lobe. It seems to be involved in planning movement.

Premotor cortex – part of the brain that resides in the frontal lobe and seems to affect physical movement.

Evidence that the brain allows for free will

Sirigu led a study in 2009 for the Cognitive Neuroscience Centre in Bron, France, that investigated the functions of different areas of the brain. The research involved experimentation on seven patients who were undergoing brain surgery to remove tumours. These patients were conscious and were able to report their experiences.

Sirigu and her team stimulated two areas of the brain with probes:

Premotor cortex	Parietal cortex
When stimulated, movement occurred but it was involuntary.	With weak stimulation, patients felt the desire to move (roll their tongue, move fingers or arms).
Patients were unaware and even denied having moved.	With strong stimulation, patients reported having moved yet researchers witnessed no movement.
Feeds back the results of the instructions to the **parietal cortex**.	Generates predictions about possible movements. Selects and sends instructions to the **premotor cortex**.

The discoveries demonstrated that the two regions work together in bringing about movement. It also might imply several things about our free will:

- that the place in the brain where the free decision can be made to act has been identified
- that the parietal cortex is responsible for 'selecting' behaviour from a range of choices
- or alternatively, that the decision to act is *not* free at all because it is stimulated (caused) by a material event. (The sensation that we will to do something could be illusory, the neurons fire, then we feel an urge to act.)

> **Typical mistake**
>
> Sirigu is not a libertarian scholar and is not arguing that this is proof that we are free. Her research has shown us where in the brain the sensation of 'free will' resides. Philosophically, we can interpret this as evidence for free will, or we could use it to confirm a belief in determinism.

> **Now test yourself**   TESTED ☐
>
> 1 Which part of the brain gave patients the sensation that they had moved?
> 2 What was the other part of the brain responsible for once stimulated?
> 3 Why has this been interpreted to mean we have free will?

> **Revision tip**
>
> Look up and copy a picture of the lobes of the brain and label the areas concerned in Sirigu's research. Make a list on your diagram of what each part did under experimentation and what they seem responsible for.

Psychological: Rogers   REVISED ☐

> **Who is Carl Rogers?**
> Rogers (1902–1987) was an award-winning American psychologist. He embraced atheism, abandoned the ministry and became known for his person-centred approach to psychology.

Humanist approach

Rogers acknowledged that conditioning affects us, especially during our childhood experiences. A developing child requires:

1 Genuineness (permission to explore their own ideas)
2 Acceptance (unconditional love)
3 Empathy (understanding)

Without these three things, a child conforms to conditioning.

But Rogers rejected behaviourism and any necessary determinism. Our behaviour emerges from our own unique perception of ourselves and our situation. His **humanistic** concept of 'the self' refers to who we really are as a person.

- Each person is unique.
- We all develop differently according to our personality.
- The self is composed of three unique concepts:
  1 Self-worth – our value
  2 Self-image – what we think we are like
  3 Ideal self – our constantly changing goals
- We want to behave in line with our self-image.

> **Humanism** – concerned with the whole person as a unique individual. It is based on the subjective unique experiences of the individual.
>
> **Self-actualisation** – for our self-image to match our ideal image (to be the person we want to be).

Self-actualisation

We have one basic motive – the desire to **self-actualise**. This means to fulfil our potential by getting our self-image to reflect our ideal self.

This requires:
- overriding the conditioning we received in early life
- becoming fully functioning persons
- being completely in touch with our feelings and experiences in the present moment.

Becoming a fully functioning person is not a process that we can complete. It is a continuous journey, not a destination. Rogers gave five characteristics of a fully functioning person:

1 Open to all experiences (both positive and negative)
2 Existential living (no preconceptions or judgements)
3 Trust feelings (listen to our intuition)
4 Creative (not always playing safe)
5 Fulfilled life (happy and satisfied)

Freedom is necessary to be a fully functioning human being. People are unique, unpredictable, reactive and free.

Now test yourself

TESTED ☐

1 In what way does Rogers accept conditioning?
2 How can we overcome our conditioning?
3 What is meant by self-actualisation?

Apply your knowledge

Hinterland is a Welsh 'whodunnit' series. In episode one, Helen Jenkins is murdered after having supervised children at a care home in Devil's Bridge. Watch the first episode/series and answer the questions below (or use any whodunnit of your choice).
1 Does any character act in bad faith during the murder inquiry?
2 How can Sirigu's research explain the murderer's actions?
3 How would Rogers account for the behaviour of the children in care?
4 Does the libertarian position allow us to punish Helen Jenkins' killer?

Revision activity

In pairs, create a set of libertarianism taboo cards using key words from this topic. Include a 'taboo' word and a list of three associated words that you cannot say. You have a minute to describe each 'taboo' word for your partner to guess.

Exam checklist

Can you:
- define existentialism
- account for our freedom with reference to 'the gap'
- explain why free will is unpleasant
- give the waiter example
- define bad faith
- explain Sirigu's research
- give the reactions from the various parts of the brain
- state the various implications concerning freedom from the experiments
- define humanism
- define the parts of the self
- explain how to achieve self-actualisation
- state the characteristics of a fully functioning person?

4F The implications of libertarianism and free will

The implications of libertarianism on moral responsibility

REVISED

If libertarians are correct, the theory influences belief regarding the responsibility of human beings for moral decisions and behaviour. It is not a clear case that if we are free, we are responsible.

The worth of human ideas of rightness, wrongness and moral value

Sartre claimed that the only ideas of right or wrong and moral value that matter are yours. There are no objective rules or guidance that we can fall back on. His conclusion was that you and only you are responsible for the actions and choices that you make – you have ultimate responsibility.

There is worth:	There is no worth:
My human ideas of right and wrong mean that I can create a decision by myself for myself. It is an act of creation and its value is intrinsic as it comes from me alone.	Moral value and community ideas of right and wrong hold no power over us and we act in bad faith when we behave as though they are authoritative.

Francis Collins (1950–present day) rejects what he calls 'Genes R Us' biological determinism. The genetic evidence presented through twin and gender studies demonstrates that we are all very different despite our genetic make-up. We are free, and thus if society tells us we have performed an action that contravenes what is acceptable, then we must take responsibility for that.

Typical mistake

The implications of libertarianism on our moral responsibility are not only positive. Make sure that you understand the negative implications as well.

The value in blaming moral agents for immoral acts

Sirigu's research may have demonstrated where free will is located in the human brain, but she makes no judgement from this in terms of whether moral agents can be blamed or praised for their actions. We can infer meaning from her work in either direction:

There is value:	There is no value:
If this research has accurately identified free will in our brain, it is valuable to praise or blame people for their acts as their choices to act do come from within them.	Sirigu's research does not demonstrate free will. Scientists could control decisions made in the parietal cortex, thus causing action. There is no value in blaming an agent for caused acts.

Rene Descartes (1596–1650) claimed freedom is self-evident and innate within us. It would be illogical and thus impossible to praise or blame automatons; instead we would have to look to the causes of their actions. The perfect, created nature of humanity is capable of free or voluntary action and it is that which makes him deserve praise or blame.

Revision activity

See if you can work out how the three specification scholars might respond to all three of the issues here. You can work out both positive and negative implications for all of them.

The usefulness of normative ethics

Rogers maintained that we behave as we do because of the way we perceive our situation. No one else can know how we perceive, so we are the best experts on ourselves. If a child is raised in a nurturing environment, or if we are given the opportunity to self-actualise, we are free.

It is useful:	It is not useful:
Situation Ethics or egoism provide individuals with a good environment, a healthy self-concept and freedom in their decision-making so they can realise their full potential.	Natural Law or Divine Command instil excessive constraints. They prevent an agent from becoming fully functioning, the ideal self being at odds with their actual behaviour.

Immanuel Kant (1724–1804) argued that moral laws are based on **a priori synthetic reasoning**. These laws are objective, and their existence is logical only if we have freedom to obey or disobey them. If one says, 'you ought not to steal', it implies that you can choose to steal or not. Thus, normative ethics are useful and meaningful only if you are free. It is a postulate of practical reason.

> **Revision tip**
>
> Read the exam question carefully. If you get a question asking you to explain the implications of libertarianism on moral responsibility, don't get bogged down in writing all you know on libertarianism. Your focus should be on the value, worth and usefulness of morality if we are really free.

> **A priori synthetic reasoning** – reasoning that begins in the mind alone, but then is applied to the empirical world.

Now test yourself   TESTED

1 Why does Sartre reject human ideas of right and wrong?
2 How does Sirigu's research suggest that praise and blame could be valuable?
3 Why might Rogers find normative ethics useful?

The implications of free will on religious belief

REVISED

If religious ideas of free will are correct, this has a significant effect on what it is logical to believe about God, his nature and the meaning or significance of our lives now.

The link between God and evil

If we are free beings, this leads to several possible conclusions regarding the link between God and evil.

There is no link	There is a link	There is a weak link
Evil originates in humans Or Evil does not exist, it is illusory.	God is responsible for: ● creating natural evil ● giving us the ability to perform moral evil.	God created natural evil: ● to enable real freedom ● as a just punishment. God gave us moral evil: ● to enable free choices ● to teach us to be more like him.

Arminius' teaching on God's foreknowledge and prevenient, resistible grace means that we are responsible for evil and saved through co-operation with God. This leads us to the following possible conclusions:

There is no link:	There is a link:
God has no power over our moral actions as we have free will. In this case, he does not will evil or bring it about; it is all our responsibility.	God is sovereign over everything; he permits and limits evil without causing or willing it. God allows evil, so we can be truly free.

Apply your knowledge

Watch an episode of *The 100*. In each episode, the characters are forced to make difficult moral choices in extreme situations.
1 Where do the characters get their moral values from?
2 If Clarke and the others are free, do they need any normative ethics?
3 What do you think it would say about God if he allowed these kinds of actions as part of his creation?

The implications for God's omnipotence and omnibenevolence

If we are free beings, this has an impact upon God's character.

God is not omnipotent if:	God is not omnibenevolent if:
• he cannot remove evil from the world • we (not he) act to save ourselves • he could only create the world this way • we can choose to turn away from his will.	• he created a world with built-in suffering • he gave us the capacity to harm each other • he allows the suffering of innocents • he foreknew this when he gave us free will.

However:

God could be powerful if he:	God could be loving if:
• preserves free will by allowing evil • limits himself by refraining from interfering with our choices.	• his gift of freedom is the best thing for us • justice for innocent suffering was served elsewhere.

Pelagius' teaching that we do not inherit original sin means divine reward or punishment is based on our own free actions. This could lead to the following possible conclusions:

God is not omnipotent or omnibenevolent:	God is omnipotent and omnibenevolent:
• God cannot save anyone who suffers unless they acted well. • Christ is powerless to save without humanity choosing him.	• God is good not arbitrary; he allows salvation to all deserving people. • God has power – his grace helps us to reach salvation at the end of life.

The use of prayer and the existence of miracles

Religious people believe:
- God answers the prayers of those who freely ask him for help
- God has the power to intervene in the natural course of events.

But this raises a few questions in the light of our free will:

1 Don't miracles interfere with our free will?
2 What happens if two people pray for opposing things?
3 If God answers prayers or performs miracles, why doesn't he do it more frequently?
4 What is the point in praying if God avoids answering to preserve our freedom?

Richard Swinburne (1934–present day) says:
- If God violates a natural law to perform a miracle, it must be for a divine reason.
- If he does so, it must be rare to avoid compromising our free will.
- To require God to reduce evil effects, yet retain our freedom, is to desire a 'toy world' where there are no opportunities for real decision-making.

Keith Ward (1938–present day) says:
- God is unchanging, and omniscient, so prayer does not inform or persuade him.
- Prayer is about bringing oneself in line with God's will, to freely become more like him.
- He does not force us to be like him as that would affect our freedom.

Now test yourself

TESTED ☐

1 How could Arminius defend God from being the author of evil?
2 How does Pelagius retain God's goodness if humans are free?
3 Why might prayer be seen as useless if humans are free beings?

Exam checklist

Can you:
- show both sides of the debate from:
  - Sartre
  - Sirigu
  - Rogers
- understand how each of them argues for or against:
  - the worth of human ideas of rightness, wrongness and moral value
  - the value in blaming moral agents for immoral acts
  - the usefulness of normative ethics
- show both sides of the debate from:
  - Arminius
  - Pelagius
- understand how each of them argues for or against:
  - the link between God and evil
  - the implication for God's omnipotence and omnibenevolence
  - the use of prayer and the existence of miracles?

Issues for analysis and evaluation

There are six issues for analysis and evaluation listed on the specification as examples of the kinds of AO2 questions you could be asked. Begin by considering the possible conclusions to the question before you establish your lines of reasoning. Develop these lines of argument by giving examples or evidence to demonstrate their points.

How convincing are religious views on free will?

REVISED ☐

Religious views on free will are very convincing	Religious views on free will are not convincing at all	Religious views on free will are appealing, not convincing
Pelagius' view is convincing as it is consistent with solutions to the problem of evil.	Pelagius failed to convince two Popes and three councils of bishops.	It is consistent with our experience, but not with church teaching.
Arminius' view is convincing as it manages to allow for both free will and predestination.	Free will and predestination are incompatible, so Arminius is incoherent.	Arminius would solve the problem but compromises the divine quality of omnipotence.
Free will ensures that divine punishment and reward are coherent.	Free will does not solve the problem that God appears to punish the innocent.	Life seems more purposeful if we are free, but scripture is clear that God decides.
Free will ensures that the divine names are preserved, and God is worthy of worship.	Free will limits God's power to save everyone, or his power to save anyone himself.	Theological explanations of free will are attractive but predestination is simpler.

The extent to which an individual has free choice

REVISED ☐

An individual has complete free choice over their actions	An individual has no free choice; it is illusory	An individual has free will within some parameters
If Pelagius is correct, then we can be said to be completely free to choose God or not.	If God is truly God, he must have the power over us that Calvin taught.	We can be free to choose the mundane in life, but it makes no difference in the end.
We make our own choices without guidance or control of any external agencies.	We are products of programming by genes and society. Nothing we do is free.	Our complex brains can utilise a wide range of influences to make 'free' decisions.
Moral exhortations make sense only if we have the power to reject them or obey them.	We only reject or obey moral commands because we are programmed to do so.	Clearly, we cannot be said to be completely free since we cannot sprout wings and fly.
We make ourselves from moment to moment through the choices that we make.	We cannot control our feelings or desires, so God or another agent is responsible for those.	To freely choose something requires the limitation of some other possibilities.

The extent to which philosophical, scientific and/or psychological views on libertarianism inevitably lead people to accept libertarianism

Libertarianism is indisputable in light of the evidence	There is nothing convincing in libertarian arguments	The evidence for freedom is compelling, not indisputable
Experimentation performed under controlled conditions produced repeatable results.	Sirigu's work demonstrates nothing about free will, only about brain structure.	It is attractive to think that part of the brain evaluates and selects without external cause.
Philosophically, it makes sense to say that a new-born baby is a blank slate.	Sartre's existentialism makes no sense. Genetic mapping shows we are not tabula rasa.	Freedom fits with human experience but so does causation.
Rogers' reputation makes it seem arrogant to dispute that we are as free as he claims.	Rogers' psychological work is not demonstrable scientifically so has no real evidence.	It helps our emotional and mental stability to believe that we are free.
There is evidence from many disciplines to suggest freedom and we have experience of it.	The scientific basis for determinism is convincing because it is repeatable.	We must accept the libertarian arguments because otherwise life seems pointless.

The extent to which free moral agents should follow normative ethics

Normative ethics are useful guides, they are not restrictive	Normative ethics are useless if we are truly free	Normative ethics restrict our freedom as moral agents
They can guide us, but they don't control us because we are free to choose.	They offer no concrete guidance at all as they are subjective ideas.	They take the form of coercive laws that we must take the time to challenge.
They make sense only if we are free to reject them, so they offer guidance not control.	They are based on someone else's values, not the ones we are making for ourselves.	They don't prevent free action, but they lay out parameters for acceptable choices.
They can foster a healthy environment for a child, to enable free decision-making.	They relate to nothing objective and cannot be trusted as a guide.	They control us and prevent us from self-actualisation when they dictate behaviour.
They are based on past experience from other free decision-making humans.	If we make ourselves, then the experience of others is of no value to us.	They begin as useful guides but become dogma and force us to submit or fight.

The degree to which free will makes the use of prayer irrelevant

Prayer makes no sense if we are free moral agents	Prayer is essential in a world where we are free agents	Prayer is about a relationship with God, not control by him
God cannot answer our prayers without compromising some part of human freedom.	A prayer, freely made, is one which consents to God's interference.	Prayer is deliberation about our place in the world, not asking God to take over.
Prayers concerning other people require the use of force by God if he is to answer.	Prayer is worshipping God because we choose to, not because we want things.	Prayer is about freely changing ourselves, not others, to make us become more like God.
Prayer reduces the world to a toy, where poor decisions are moot as God will fix them.	If we have responsibility, we need prayer to aid careful consideration before we act.	Prayer cannot be used to control God's actions as he is not determined either.
Real freedom is distance from knowledge of God, so he cannot respond to prayer.	Prayer is real communication with a personal God. This can happen only if we are free.	Communication requires both parties to respond to, not control, each other.

The degree to which beliefs about free will can be reconciled with beliefs about predestination

REVISED ☐

Free will makes no sense if we are predestined by God	Free will and predestination are completely compatible	Some readings of free will and predestination are compatible
If God foreknows what we will do, then we cannot be considered free to choose.	God is both powerful and good, so he is in control, and we deserve our punishments.	Arminius' foreknowledge is no less limiting than if God caused our actions.
Any 'free' actions are meaningless if God has decided our final destination.	We are only free to sin. This means we can choose freely, but we will only choose evil.	An understanding of God as first cause makes him responsible for who we are.
Humans are not self-determining if God created our soul or essence.	All the religious scholars have both free will and predestination in their thinking.	God as creator ex nihilo conflicts with the idea of humans as completely free.
Foreknowledge suggests fixity of action; this means that freedom is, at best, an illusion.	Our perspective is limited. An omnipotent God can foreknow what we freely will do.	Foreknowledge works if God exists outside time and space. His perspective is different.

Specimen exam questions

Sample AO1 questions

1 Compare the religious concepts of free will from Pelagius and Arminius.
2 Examine the philosophical defence of libertarianism from Sartre.
3 Explain the main arguments for libertarianism.
4 Explain the implications of libertarianism on moral responsibility.
5 Examine why Arminius rejected the Calvinist view of predestination.

> **Revision tip**
>
> Be prepared to have to show the similarities and differences between the specification scholars.

Sample AO2 questions

1 Evaluate the view that prayer is pointless if humans are completely free.
2 'Human beings have complete free choice.' Evaluate this view.

> **Revision tip**
>
> It is vital that you can refer to arguments from both libertarian and determinist scholars in an AO2 question.